For Ted
with best wishes
John

Multiple Realities in Clinical Practice

Multiple Realities in Clinical Practice

JOHN S. KAFKA, M . D .

Yale University Press New Haven and London

Published with assistance from the foundation established in memory of William McKean Brown.

Designed by James J. Johnson
and set in Times Roman type
by Keystone Typesetting, Inc., Orwigsburg, Pennsylvania.
Printed in the United States of America by Vail-Ballou Press, Binghamton, New York.

Library of Congress Cataloging-in-Publication Data

Kafka, John S., 1921–
    Multiple realities in clinical practice / John S. Kafka.
        p. cm.
    Bibliography: p.
    Includes index.
    ISBN 0–300–04350–3 (alk. paper)
    1. Psychoanalysis. 2. Reality. I. Title.
    [DNLM: 1. Psychoanalytic Therapy. WM 460.6 K11m]
RC506.K33 1989
616.89′17—dc19
DNLM/DLC
for Library of Congress   88–38238
                                                                CIP

The paper in this book meets the guidelines for permanence and durability of the Committee on Production Guidelines for Book Longevity of the Council on Library Resources.

10 9 8 7 6 5 4 3 2 1

*To Marian, David Egon, Paul Henry,
and Alexander Charles*

Contents

Acknowledgments

Several years ago, at the invitation of Professor Helmut Thomä, I served as visiting professor at the University of Ulm in West Germany. Professor Horst Kächele urged me persistently and enthusiastically to develop more fully in a book ideas that I had summarized in some lectures. The Breuninger Foundation then named me the first recipient of the senior (psychoanalytic) scientist award and provided some financial support. I want to express my gratitude to the Breuninger Foundation and to Dr. Helga Breuninger personally for the support and encouragement that contributed to the eventual realization of this project.

I want to acknowledge the early parental and family influences on some attitudes reflected in the book. I am thankful to my patients for all they have taught me. The teachers and supervisors I remember with special gratitude are those who did not hide a measured skepticism vis-à-vis some accepted views. I owe much to my students and supervisees, to my teachers at the University of Chicago, Emory and Yale universities, and elsewhere, and current and past colleagues in many settings, including the Washington Psychoanalytic Society and Institute, Chestnut Lodge, the National Institute of Mental Health, and George Washington University School of Medicine. Since this book reflects multiple aspects of my life and thought, I would like to thank more individuals than is possible and I therefore reluctantly mention only those institutions. Drs. Edoardo Weiss, Winifred Whitman, Harold Searles, Otto Will, Edith Weigert, and Robert Cohen, however, played very specific roles in some aspects of my training. Many teachers influenced me profoundly, but Drs. Lawrence Kubie and Hans Loewald were among those whose psychoanalytic thinking influenced me significantly prior to my formal psychoanalytic training.

In connection with the content of the book, I gratefully acknowledge Dr. Kenneth Gaarder's role in the LSD work and his central role in the Sernyl research. Although the responsibility for the formulations offered is mine, a passage in the book concerning families of hospitalized patients reflects cooperative work with Joyce McDonald. Some passages reflect work done in cooperation with Dr. Hedda Bolgar and others are related to work with Dr. Robert Ryder. Some passages that reflect specific cooperation with Dr. Marian S. Kafka are indicated in the body of the book. There was, however, not only collaborative work with my wife in a specific area. While it is customary to thank one's spouse for a generally supportive atmosphere, I encountered lively and critical engagement with my ideas on the part of my family, my wife and our three sons, to whom this book is dedicated.

I want to thank the Yale-appointed readers of the manuscript for critical comments and suggestions. My gratitude to Gladys Topkis for being the essential encouraging and helpful guide in the preparation of this book, to Gloria Parloff for her outstanding editorial work, which combined understanding of the project and a perspective of the whole work with careful attention to detail, and to the manuscript editor, Cecile Watters. My thanks to my long-time assistant and secretary, Dorothy Streett, who helped in innumerable ways, and to Dr. David Mandelkern, Kyung-Sook Lee, and Shen O. Chen for their parts in the preparation of the manuscript.

Grateful acknowledgment is made to the following for permission to reprint published material: the Continuum Publishing Company, for an excerpt from *The Innerworld of the Outerworld of the Innerworld,* translated by Michael Roloff, translation © 1974 by

Michael Roloff, reprinted by permission; the Psychological Corporation, in behalf of Grune and Stratton, Inc., for material from *Current Psychiatric Therapies,* vol. 5, ed. Jules H. Masserman; International Universities Press, Inc., for material from *Psychoanalysis and Psychosis,* ed. Ann-Louise S. Silver; Jason Aronson, Inc., for material from *The Dream in Clinical Practice,* ed. J. M. Natterson; and the Analytic Press, for material from "The schizophrenic's objects: Implications for treatment strategies," in *Towards a Comprehensive Model for Schizophrenic Disorders: Psychoanalytic Essays in Memory of Ping-Nie Pao, M.D.,* ed. D. B. Feinsilver, copyright © 1986 by the Analytic Press.

Multiple Realities in Clinical Practice

Introduction

The conviction that we all share a commonsense reality is the basis of ordinary daily communication. Although we are aware of the fluidity of our perceptions, we operate in our daily lives with confidence that we can agree on certain self-evident structural stabilities in our physical world. This physical world provides the base of our commonsense psychological realities; it is the medium in which our communications and the expression of our needs and wants take place. We have confidence that we can return from our dreams and our flights of fancy to the common ground of commonsense reality. We cannot take this ability for granted in some of our patients, however, and we may describe the degree to which their *reality-testing* capacity is or is not intact. Our patients alert us to the mechanisms by which reality or realities are constructed and evaluated, the *sense* of reality strengthened and weakened. We encounter the phenomenon of *derealization* with its *uncanny* affective component of being *not of this world*, the affect of dread.

The processes that lead to our shared commonsense reality, processes that include socialization, are absorbing and complex. As we study them, however, and look more closely at the development of our knowledge of the world, at epistemology, it dawns on us that this admittedly essential common ground of our common-sense reality may be narrower than we had thought. Only a subtle and highly differentiated spoken or unspoken language can do justice to our rich personal realities, whereas an analogy can perhaps be made between the essential, but limited, ground covered by commonsense reality and the world that can be described in Pidgin English.

Most of us are aware at times of discrepancies between our own reality perceptions and those of others. Such discrepancies sometimes do, but often do not, present a problem for us. Patients, however, even those whose reality testing is not in question, bring to our consulting rooms the problematic aspects of such discrepancies. It is not sufficient for them to share with others the common ground of commonsense reality. They have a need to include in the realities in which they move and function some terrain extending beyond these narrow limits. Whether they know it or not, they seek a therapist with a wider stance, one who conveys a feeling that he or she is ready to encompass, potentially at least, a wider and widening reality, even if its eventual forms and dimensions are yet uncertain. A significant portion of the psychoanalyst's work reaches beyond *understanding* (providing a common base and platform that *stands under* the currently shared realities) to *comprehending*, *encompassing*, and *widening* his reality perceptions. If the psychoanalyst implicitly conveys to the patient the readiness to expand his own reality perceptions, the patient will sense that he may not be alone in both his current and his developing worlds. This book, therefore, is about the expanding framework for *comprehension*, the inclusion of different organizations of reality, organizations that have their own developmental patterns and rhythms.

As a therapy, psychoanalysis differs from other approaches by aiming not only at change or elimination of symptoms but at changes that are organically related to the individual's comprehension—whether or not such comprehension finds a pathway to conscious verbal expression—of the origin and function of symptoms, defenses, character structures, and ways of perceiving the world. This book is thus also about the process of psychological change, and that signifies a change in the perception of what things *mean.* Our realities on close examination are precisely that: *what things mean.*

Although psychoanalysis has always been concerned with psychic reality, most clinical psychoanalysts, on the one hand, justifiably distrust armchair philosophizing, especially of the vaguely existential kind, and, on the other hand, are often not in touch with some relevant experimental work on perception and cognition. Yet it is precisely clinical work that constantly brings one in contact with questions about the nature of knowledge, questions of how convictions, with their cognitive and affective charges, are formed and changed. Unless his philosophobia causes him to slam the door shut a priori, the clinician must confront some epistemological issues. Thus, finally, this book considers some of these clinically based questions about the nature of knowledge.

I will write about my understanding and treatment of neurotic and psychotic patients, about a clinician's perspective on some broad epistemological questions, and about the contributions, in turn, of epistemological insights to clinical issues. The constant interplay between clinical and theoretical work sometimes gives the analytic office its most peculiar stamp, that of a laboratory of philosophy. Some organizing themes have emerged in the course of this work, hypotheses about how multiple-reality organizations evolve through affectively determined perceptual processes and how temporal phenomena occupy a central place in our efforts to understand mind.

A major aspect of the psychoanalyst's training consists in uncovering the roots of his or her own ways of perceiving and relating to the world and the origin and context of personal values. Such self-knowledge plays a major role in the formation of the analyst's attitude of not imposing perceptions and values on the analysand, to avoid "contamination" and to facilitate the blossoming of genuine autonomy. The reader of an analyst's writings, however, may be helped in the understanding and critical evaluation of the ideas put forward by knowing something about the author. After all, the major themes that characterize the writings of a psychoanalyst are rooted in his life and work experience, and their development can best be understood in the context of his scientific autobiography.

In one sense, the multiple-reality theme entered my life quite early. The first thirteen years in Austria, the next six in France, and the years since then in the United States confronted me with different cultural realities, which, to a significant degree, I had to make my own. The tempo of these different settings impressed me forcefully. I have vivid memories of the heavy um-pah rhythm of a Tyrolean band that was playing at a railway station when I left Austria and of the almost frantic tempo of a quick-stepping "Chasseurs Alpins" band that marched past the railway station at my first stop in France. My focus on tempo and time had early roots, and a teacher in France who presented Henri Bergson's work beautifully and enthusiastically helped my ideational elaboration of vaguely felt preoccupations. To the necessity of dealing with different ethnic realities and tempos was added the necessity of living, and making a living, at very different socioeconomic levels—as a student in Europe, a laborer in my first years in the United States, and then as a student again, moving from the humanities to psychology, to medicine, to psychiatry and psychoanalysis. All this further prepared the ground for my preoccupation with multiple realities.

Although I did not initially plan specifically to investigate an area labeled "multiple realities," the theme emerged in various guises as I moved on my personal voyage from one phase of my life to another. As a student, as a psychoanalyst, as a research psychiatrist, and as a person with the usual human curiosity, I found that the limited areas on which my attention was customarily focused began to coalesce into broader formulations. Throughout, an openness to philosophical and epistemological thinking shaped the context of my developing perspective.

The work of Heinrich Klüver, one of my teachers at the University of Chicago, seemed to deal directly with the rigorous study of multiple psychological realities. His approach, to which I shall return on several occasions in the body of this book, involved the study of sets of different physical stimuli that the organism treats as subjectively equivalent. His work can inform and enrich even a clinical understanding of the concept of object constancy.

It is, of course, the psychotic patient who most strikingly lives in a different reality. The description of the consulting room as a laboratory of philosophy is particularly apt here. Epistemology changes from an abstract discipline to one of literally vital importance for the psychiatrist who refuses to accept the idea that psychotics "do not make sense." The awareness of different reality organizations is the essential tool of the therapist treating psychotic patients. Although these problems forced themselves on me first in my work with such patients, I later learned how much the awareness of different reality organizations is also a useful—in my view, essential—instrument in the treatment of nonpsychotic patients. I have become increasingly convinced that in most instances in which psychoanalysis is carried to an appropriate depth, the changes in subjective reality are such that issues of reality perception are pertinent. In this book I will elaborate on the theme that a simple-minded distinction between cognitive and affective functions is erroneous. I will describe how I have come to view cognitive and perceptual processes as in their very essence affectively informed and determined.

Psychoanalysis was not the first therapy with which I became acquainted. Carl Rogers was among my early teachers; despite my appreciation of the man and the useful components of his approach to therapy, its inherent limitations made me look elsewhere, and my search led me to psychoanalytic training. I have often been struck by the degree of disappointment shown by some colleagues whose only therapeutic training was in psychoanalysis when they discovered flaws or limitations in psychoanalytic theory or technique. It was relatively easy for me to take these limitations for granted since I could contrast the richness offered within the psychoanalytic framework with approaches I had previously encountered. I found room here for the progressive development of my ideas concerning multiple realities and their application to the study of family structure and the treatment of neurotic patients—those with character disorders or borderline personality structure—and, within limits that will be spelled out, psychotic patients.

Symptom-oriented treatment facilities are currently fashionable, at least in the United States. There are, for example, separate anxiety clinics, depression clinics, phobia clinics. The interest in psychotherapeutic approaches to the psychoses is at a low ebb, although some lip service is given to the need for psychotherapeutic work in conjunction with psychopharmacological treatment. Nevertheless, increasing numbers of investigators and clinicians have a sophisticated nonreductionistic approach to what is essentially the mind-body problem as it is encountered in our field. An argument could perhaps be made that the rapid progress in the biology of the central nervous system has so far led to more understanding of the biological events "connected" to "normal" psychological processes—perception, affect, and thought—than to the biology of psychopathology. Increasing understanding of the enormous plasticity of the central nervous system makes plausible the idea that specific stresses during specific developmental phases can lead to biologically definable changes. And not only may questions of etiology be clarified but the effective range and limitations of psychotherapeutic interventions may be better defined. The study of mechanisms of memory may be particularly pertinent here (Squire, 1986). In any case, it is my belief that most clinicians operate nowadays with some rudimentary formulations about "biology."

Thoughts about the biology of perception form a background for some of my formulations, and I will attempt to make them explicit. My tentative model of the schizophrenic disorders, for instance, specifies an area in which biological explanations may be pertinent. My focus in this context is not on the philosophical mind-body problem as such but on the conscious model that informs the clinician's operations and may also determine research strategies at a time when one is forced to operate with an admittedly incomplete model. The broadly conceived model of schizophrenic disorders that will be presented gives a prominent place to perceptual processes and to questions of sensory compartmentalization versus synesthetic phenomena. For such a model, biological research dealing with neurotransmitters and receptors involved in localization and spread of nervous impulses is pertinent. This may be the case even if the broader model utilizes concepts such as "conflict," "impulse," and "drive."

A preoccupation with the question of what size organism is the most appropriate unit of study characterizes my work and represents a theme with multiple roots and multiple ramifications. On the more clinical level, questions of preference for therapeutic focus on the individual, the family, or the group are related to more theoretical questions about the optimal size of the psychobiological unit to be studied. There may not, however, be an absolute correspondence between the most informative unit size for purposes of the theoretical study of specific questions and the optimal unit size for therapeutic application. For me, the interest in the question of appropriate unit size has coexisted with and informed my therapeutic focus on the individual. It may even have strengthened this focus. The gradual sharpening of my idea that temporal rather than spatial dimensions are the more promising topics of study in our field may have played a part here. In retrospect, it is conceivable that the possibilities of optimal temporal, rhythmic resonance between individual therapist and individual patient may have influenced my decision to focus on one-to-one therapeutic and psychoanalytic work, although I have worked with couples, families, and groups and occasionally still do so.

Spatial models of mental structures, it seems to me, carry more danger of reification, and thus I have been increasingly concerned with the possibilities of expressing ideas in temporal terms, with issues of appropriate temporal units and problems of temporal expansion and contraction in psychic life. My preoccupation with time has alternated between two polarities, although I have attempted to construct a connecting bridge. One polarity is clinical, phenomenological, and experimental; the other—although I have reservations about the use of the term here—is more "philosophical." Connected with the first polarity is a focus on temporal aspects of perceptual processes—the notion that each perceptual act recapitulates the ontogeny of perception. This idea, which has clinical and experimental underpinnings and also significant diagnostic and therapeutic implications, will be developed in the body of the book. Let us note, however, that if the infant's early perceptual discriminations involve the distinction between what is inside and outside his body (in other words, the establishment of the size of the organism), the distinctions between animate and inanimate objects and between characteristics that ultimately lead to the differentiation of the spatial and temporal dimensions, then these distinctions, rapidly recapitulated in each adult perceptual act, represent the axes along which realities are organized.

Because of the complexities of the idea of perceptual recapitulation, unfamiliarity with the notion that the history of the development of perception is unrolled in each perceptual act, I would like to introduce here the more familiar description of another recapitulative experience. It is said that individuals confronting sudden mortal danger often experience a rapid rerun of their whole previous life. This recapitulation of the "perception" of one's life, described as conveying a sense of completeness and including a reexperience of emotional change and evolution, is highly condensed and packaged into an unbelievably short time span. I believe that traumatic conditions are not essential for this phenomenon to occur and that even in ordinary circumstances each perception involves a recapitulation of its development. The affective and therefore the transferential history is also packaged in this recapitulation. The preconscious richness of our affectively informed contact with ourselves and with the world depends on and derives from the overtones of recapitulation and condensation, the constant rapid replay of our cognitive and emotional histories. What distinguishes individuals facing mortal danger is that they are conscious of such recapitulation. The experience of time at such a juncture will also be a topic of major interest.

My overarching concern with time is not limited to such issues as the recapitulation of ontogeny, the development of perception in each perceptual act. Although I do not start with an explicit philosophical position (or philosophy of science), the more "philosophical" polarity of my preoccupation with time rather than space is related to the zeitgeist derived from modern physics. Psychoanalysts, I believe, have timidly neglected the insight of modern physics that, in order to understand certain phenomena, one must understand the relationships among matter, time, and energy rather than merely the commonsense meanings of these terms. Such an insight may be pertinent to our field. Biology, too, emphasizes systems of energy rather than commonsense matter—for example, in discussions by molecular biologists of the nature of cell membranes. I will examine models of the nervous system based on temporal rather than spatial characteristics. I will argue that the focus on time permits a new perspective on the mind-body problem and perhaps makes less shocking Hans Loewald's radical statement that "time is the fiber of mind." Focus on temporal structure, as I hope to demonstrate, has immediate and practical effects on clinical work. The issue of the size of the organism seems to be anchored in a reified spatial dimension, but even a cursory examination of that question dispels the idea: the individual who sees himself as part of a group at that moment changes his temporal perspective, since the unit that contributes to his "reality" may well extend beyond his individual life span. The moments of maternal-infant fusion are perhaps the most obvious examples of temporally different reality.

Order and structure are topics in which clinical and philosophical preoccupations meet. In clinical psychoanalysis we encounter the word *structure* in the context of "structural change." The study of change in psychoanalysis and an examination of the concept of structure in this context have led me to another facet of the multiple-reality theme. A retrospective view of cases in which significant change, perhaps structural change, occurred led to the discovery that such cases were characterized by a change from animate to inanimate features of "objects" encountered in the analytic work. This observation in turn led to the following question: can the analysand's experience of objects changing, on a symbolic level, from animate to inanimate and vice versa—a change in the relationship to objects—be connected to the perceptual discrimination between the animate and the inanimate, and even to the infant's development of this differentiation? It would indeed be intriguing if a connection could be established between "structural" change in the psychoanalytic sense—the shift from "insight" to "active" change—and the early distinction between the animate and inanimate worlds. The possible pertinence here of the work of the physicist Ilya Prigogine on structural changes will be discussed. There is also much current interest in "state-specific" learning, a topic akin to Paul Federn's separate "ego states." I will explore the possibility that these different ego states may be characterized by the different animate or inanimate structures. I will propose that the "entitlement" of certain narcissistic patients is related to their lack of differentiation of the animate and inanimate.

The ability to treat the same object as both animate and inanimate is often discussed in a developmental framework and related to Winnicott's work on transitional objects. My emphasis on the creative and therapeutic uses of a multiple reality that encompasses the realities of the same object as both animate and inanimate and my critique and reformulation of double-bind theory have considerable affinity with Winnicott's work. My thesis is that intolerance of ambiguity (including the ambiguity concerning the animate and inanimate nature of objects) rather than paradoxical communication tends to be pathogenic. Compared to the relative stability of the inanimate world—it is fixed in place, *in space*— the movement of animate beings—the ability to change position and attitude from moment to moment—emphasizes its *temporal* characteristics. My own extension or elaboration of the transitional realm between the animate and inanimate worlds introduces the notion of the transitional between the spatial (or "material") and the temporal—an idea that bears some relationship to Gilbert Rose's extension of the transitional experience to the "transitional process" (1980). In discussing transitional experience I will also take into account that the animate being has temporal intentionality—orientation toward the future. One may speak of an animate directionality, but even the animate being may experience the past as being fixed, as being experientially unchanging and therefore quasi-spatial, less temporal. Experientially the past may be associated with deanimated "deposits" until the latter are revitalized, reanimated because their meaning—brought into new contexts because of life events or by psychoanalytic reactivation—*changes*, that is, enters the explicitly temporal dimension. The role of rituals in either enlivening or deadening the past will also be examined.

Awareness of the processes by which each patient forms both the more ephemeral and the more lasting aspects of his or her realities fosters in the therapist a profound respect for the validity of the individual's universe. This added respect colors the atmosphere of the consulting room and underlines the analyst's non-

judgmental stance, which is a major component of the psychoanalyst's training. The arguments that a value-free position is
unreachable in practice have led some clinicians to downplay the
importance of efforts to approximate it. In one sense, however,
psychoanalysis cannot escape the issue of morality. Psychoanalysts are determinists: antecedents determine behavior and psychoanalytic theories are invoked in the courtroom when attempts are
made to connect the criminal's upbringing with his crime. At first
glance, moral issues, "free" will, and (psychic) determinism seem
to have nothing to do with the perception of the size of the
organism. On second look, the very courtroom argument hinges
on the question of whether the appropriate unit size is the larger or
the smaller one, the family or the individual. In general, the
behavior of an organism may be "determined" if this organism
belongs to a larger one—or to an organism whose duration, whose
life span, is longer than that of its component parts. The behavior
may be seen as "free" if the organism is separate and apparently
"independent." An observer will come to different conclusions
when studying an individual ant within or without the context of its
colony. In clinical work perceptions of the size of the organism
fluctuate—individual or family, for instance—and we will explore
the connections between organisms' size and free will. Such issues
are pertinent for an understanding of the development of a sense of
autonomy in psychoanalytic treatment.

My ideas about ambiguity continued to develop when I introduced Gödel's concepts in my critique of double-bind theory
(Kafka, 1971b). At that time the idea of outside-inside ambiguity,
which is essentially another way to talk about the uncertainty of the
absolute size of an organism, began to take increasingly formal
shape for me. These ideas probably seemed more esoteric prior to
Hofstadter's popularization of Gödel (Hofstadter, 1979), but even
now they are somewhat distant from the clinician's everyday
concerns. Yet I believe that a clinical approach that reaches far
enough must deal with the organization of the individual's realities, and some propositions dealing with the nature of our realities
are formal—that is, they lie in the field of formal logic. The
difficulties lie with the clinician's prejudice regarding a humanis-

tic/scientific or philosophical/scientific dichotomy. Perhaps it is derived in part from a commonsense but antiquated mind/body dichotomy.

The development of the ideas outlined in this introduction thus involved, and continues to involve, movement from clinical practice and observation to theoretical elaboration, return to clinical work equipped with new theoretical formulations, and then further engagement in theory building—an ongoing process consisting of slow swings and rapid oscillations. This description essentially describes clinical work itself, as I understand it, and even the more theoretical formulations represent one set of traces left by such psychoanalytic or psychoanalytically informed endeavors. The back-and-forth nature of such traces to some extent limits the sequential orderliness of their presentation, and some repetition is unavoidable. I believe, however, that what is repeated in an ever-widening context becomes altered by that very process.

In what follows I will first speak of time, timing, and temporal perspective, with an emphasis on the clinical situation. Chapter 2 focuses on multiple realities in thought and object formation. In chapter 3 I will return to time and mind, after having found more solid footing in the theory developed in chapter 2. I will also in this chapter describe the development of some of my ideas during research with LSD and Sernyl in the 1960s, a time when interest in those drugs was at its height, both because of widespread experimentation with consciousness-expanding substances and because of their possible significance as keys to a better understanding of hallucinatory behavior during psychosis.

In chapter 4 the multiple-reality formulations are applied to issues of diagnosis and treatment. I will here consider the counter-transference elements embodied in the establishment of diagnostic categories and the idea that animate-inanimate confusion is limited to specific areas of conflict in some diagnostic categories and not in others. The chapter includes clinical data illustrating a connection between therapeutic structural change and alteration in the animate-inanimate discrimination dichotomy.

The focus of chapter 5 is on schizophrenia and schizophrenic thought disorder, subjects par excellence for the investigator of multiple realities. The chapter includes an excursion into the assessment of the dreams of schizophrenics—work I did some years ago in response to an invitation. At that time I recognized the fit of the paradoxical topic of the dreaming schizophrenic with my central interests: how do those whose waking reality sometimes seems so dreamlike dream?

Chapter 6 explores the widening applications of the multiple-reality approach—for example, to the study of rituals, family dynamics, and group behavior. The concluding chapter examines the compatibility of the multiple-reality emphasis with psychoanalytic theory and clinical practice and sketches the prospects that may lie ahead.

The close connection between clinical and theoretical thinking enriches a psychoanalyst's daily work. Such mutual reinforcement is the most powerful antagonist of possible burnout, and since the affect-cognition dichotomy is an artificial one, a technique well founded in theory is the basis of a genuinely humanistic therapeutic approach. For this to be so, however, there must be a personal and critical engagement with theory, an integration of theory with the broadest personal vistas. It is my hope that the presentation of my integrative efforts will contribute to the reader's individual integrative work.

Chapter I

Time, Timing, and Temporal Perspective

A hospitalized patient, Ms. R., once informed me that the earth was shrinking between the central unit of the hospital complex and the recreation building. After several days and repeated observations I realized that she was walking much faster than usual. The visibility, the touchability, of objects in space gives the spatial dimension a concreteness that the temporal dimension lacks. Somehow, for most of us, time seems to shrink and expand more easily than space. Time more easily seems and is described as "shorter" or "longer" than space even though we have to use these spatial words to describe the temporal interval. Extreme expansion of time—or the contraction of the history of a *lifetime* to fit the experienced expanding moment—may be described in retrospect by the individual who has faced mortal danger. Clearly, the priority of a "spatial" over a "temporal" reality anchor did not exist for my patient whose earth was shrinking, nor for other patients with whom I have worked. Gradually, in my efforts to understand the workings of mind, the construction of different realities, time has also assumed a position of priority.

In a psychiatric context the most common reference to the topic of time occurs in the mental-status examination. The patient is or is not "oriented in time." Every clinician has encountered patients whose time sense is profoundly disorganized but who have learned how to "pass" mental-status examinations by a variety of techniques, such as looking at the date in a newspaper or asking other patients. Clinicians have also learned techniques to counteract such "cheating." The question of the connection between temporal information and "meaningful" temporal experience surfaces immediately. The limitations of a future-oriented temporal perspective in depressed patients are perhaps the next most common psychiatric references to the topic of time. Analytic contributions, despite some increase in recent years, have been relatively scarce.

The first psychoanalytic panel on "The Experience of Time," in which I was a participant, was held at a meeting of the American Psychoanalytic Association in New York in 1971. Introducing the panel, Hans Loewald pointed out that Freud experienced frustration in his attempts to deal with the concept of time but that in psychoanalysis as a treatment procedure, as a research method, and as a body of theory, concepts and phenomena related to time are essential. Loewald reminded us just how essential they are:

> Memory, forgetting, regression, repetition, anticipation, presentation, representation, the influence on the present of the past in terms of thought, feeling, and behavior; delay of gratification, sleep-wakefulness rhythms, variations and abnormalities in the sense of elapsed time; the so-called timelessness of the id; values, standards, ideals as future-oriented categories; concepts such as object constancy and self identity—all these are central in our work. Add to this the consideration of time in the psychoanalytic process, such as schedules and the ending of hours. Furthermore, psychoanalysis is unthinkable without the theory of evolution and ontogenesis of mental development. . . . Fixation, delays, detours, arrests, and developmental spurts are major factors in shaping mental life and its disturbances. Emotional reworking of developmental factors in the present leads to more harmonious, less disturbed integration of personality and thus, to some degree, to mastery over the shape of the present and of the future. . . .
>
> How is time—objectively measured by clocks as duration—subjectively experienced? What distortions of objective world-time do we observe; how can we understand and explain them? Phenomena such as *déjà vu*, screen memories, amnesias, contractions of time in dreams and fantasies, fall under the rubric of time experience and its variations. . . . Symbolic meanings of time play a role in mental life; how do such meanings intermesh with the development of the concept of time as duration and succession

of events in physical time-space? What determines the rise of this time concept in secondary-process ideation? . . . Time can be seen in terms of reciprocal relations of past, present, and future as active modes of psychic life. In our psychoanalytic work, we discover the interaction and relation between these three temporal modes of psychic activity in the play of transference, in the impact on the present of conscious and unconscious remembering and anticipating. (Reported in Kafka, 1972, pp. 650–51)

Initially I will discuss four time-related clinical topics, some briefly and some more extensively: (1) gross temporal disorientation, (2) interpersonal timing, (3) psychoanalytic restructuring of past experience, and (4) temporal perspective.

Gross Temporal Disorientation

Gross temporal disorientation is widely recognized and discussed in the psychiatric literature. We are all sufficiently familiar with some degree of disorientation in our lives that we can appreciate some aspects of massive disorientation. Although we maintain some temporal orientation in ordinary sleep, the "time lost" under anesthesia has a more disorienting effect. Boring's courageous early research on temporal orientation perhaps deserves special mention (Boring, 1933). He awakened farmers in a quiet rural area and asked them what time it was. Then he identified himself as a researcher and inquired what cues they had used to make the temporal judgments. The sensation of fullness in the bladder was one of the major cues. Thus Boring learned that "coming to one's senses," as the term applies to time sense (temporal orientation), involves taking an inventory in which the assessment of bodily pressures, needs, and appetites apparently plays a prominent role.

That most of us seldom have to live with temporal diurnal disorientation is attested to by the fact that we are usually successful in setting our internal alarm. In the evening we decide when we wish to wake up and are often able to do so without the help of clocks. Similarly, if at times we feel much older or younger than we are, we *know* that we feel older or younger. Contrast this with certain disoriented patients, who have to live like actors in that they never know which parts of their lives they will have to incorporate into the roles they are asked to play. They resemble Billy Pilgrim, the central character in Kurt Vonnegut's novel *Slaughterhouse-Five* (1969).

> Listen: Billy Pilgrim has come unstuck in time. Billy has gone to sleep a senile widower and awakened on his wedding day. He has walked through a door in 1955 and come out another one in 1941. He has gone back through that door to find himself in 1963. He has seen his birth and death many times, he says, and pays random visits to all the events in between. He says. Billy is spastic in time, has no control over where he is going next, and the trips aren't necessarily fun. He is in a constant state of stage fright, he says, because he never knows what part of his life he is going to have to act in next. (p. 20)

The term *actor* is particularly apt, since some patients learn to act quite well. Many learn to act as though they were much less confused than they actually are. The intermittent moments of knowledge about their confusion lead to skillful defensive maneuvers. The only way they can be one up on the psychiatrist is to take advantage of the fact that sometimes they know better than he when they are "off." I am getting ahead of my story, however, a story connected with the theory that the movements in and out of psychosis are much more rapid than is generally believed. But let us now move from psychotic disorientation to a brief look at nonpsychotic daily life.

Interpersonal Timing

In the give-and-take of ordinary conversations, the timing of speech and gestures is determined in part by the speaker's assessment of the characteristics of the listener and by a complex network of mutual expectations. The better I know my friend, the more accurately I can assess his mood, his interest in a topic, his appreciation of the levels to which I carry the consideration of the topic, and the many other factors that codetermine not only what I communicate but also the rate and changes of rate of my communications. Feedback—verbal and nonverbal—constantly influences this rate. Certain patterns of unpredictability can have disorienting effects (Kafka, 1957b), and the analyst's silence and his unpredictable breaking of the silence can contribute to the mild disorientation in which temporal restructuring occurs.

Psychoanalytic Restructuring of Past Experience

The fact that the psychoanalyst observes the restructuring of past experience in the present deserves to be in the center of the picture. The analyst is interested in the effects of such restructuring on the experience of time and on temporal perspective and, conversely, in the effects of changes in time experience and perspective on the nature of such reorganization. Some experimental evidence bears on this clinical subject.

In a complex study, Ornstein (1969) demonstrated the retroactive effects of new information on judgment of past duration. His approach can be schematically indicated as follows: Subjects in one experimental group learned a series of apparently random numbers and then were asked how long it took them to learn the series. Subjects in another group learned the same series and then were given a code that transformed what was apparently a random series into an ordered one before being asked how long it took them to learn the series. The subjects who were given the code and whose actual learning period was the same estimated the learning period as shorter than did the subjects who were not given the information that would have permitted them to reorganize—recode—their experience retrospectively. It is well established that ordered numbers are learned more rapidly than random ones. Subjects given the code that transformed the apparently random series into an ordered one after learning them estimated their learning period as though they had known the ordering code at the time of learning. New information had indeed had a retroactive effect on judgment of past duration.

In an experiment some years ago (Kafka, 1957a), I studied how some persons approached the task of judging the duration of a series of intervals during which they were left—with different sets of instructions—in a darkened room with an autokinetic light. These periods were interspersed with rest intervals in a completely dark room, the duration of which they were also asked to estimate restrospectively. The responses of the experimental subjects were tape-recorded. Typically a particular interval—for instance, "the second time I was in the dark room"—was estimated first and then served as an anchor, as a reference unit, to which the others were compared as being, for instance, "a little longer" or "only about half as long" or "shorter by a third." The choice of reference intervals seemed to be related to clinically discernible moods and affects since depressively tinged affect seemed to be associated with the choice of dark reference units. This tentative finding would have to be confirmed by a predictive study. In any event, the patterns of time judgments did suggest that some overestimators who used "dark" reference intervals made larger "corrections" in arriving at estimates of "light" intervals. What does this mean? The individual makes an effort to judge the intervals correctly. He or she selects a "dark" interval as reference unit presumably because of the belief that this interval can be judged more correctly than the others. "Dark" intervals are often overestimated, and this is the case for this individual. By making a larger "correction" in arriving at estimates of "light" intervals, the experimental subject acts as if he or she knew that the "dark" interval had been overestimated, apparently using self-observation operating below awareness since the conscious decision to select the "dark" reference interval was based on the belief that it could be judged most accurately. The effort to reconcile contrasting and differentially grained experiences of duration can be studied in clinical work as well as in such a setting. (I use the term *grain* as in photographic film—the varying sizes of "now" perhaps representing temporal distance between moments of self-awareness.)

The time-related aspects of the psychoanalytic situation include the following:

1. The patient's analytic hour, his extended time-out (from work, usual activity, usual style of behavior and communicating), is the analyst's extended and relatively usual time-in.

2. The analyst, more than the patient, assumes that contiguity of communication (and of experience) has *possible* meaning implications transcending contiguity as such.

3. The analyst, more than the patient, assumes that the temporal distance of communication (and of experience) does not

eliminate the possibility of *meaningful* connection and may even be a *defense* against such connection.

4. The analyst may thus be said to be both a condenser and a dilator of time.

5. Sequence may be translated in the context of clarifications and interpretations as having specific meaning as such. Sequential dream "phrases," for instance, may be translated into prepositional clauses: dream scene A followed by dream scene B may be interpreted as "*if* A, then B."

6. The analyst, a condenser and dilator of time who attaches unusual meanings to sequences and pays strict attention to the beginning and ending of sessions, yet seems also to live in a different temporal world which he treats "loosely," may for all these reasons be seen by the patient as dealing with time in a most peculiar way.

7. The patient who finds that some of these peculiar dilating and contracting ways of looking at time are productive and meaningful in furthering insight may—by identification, by other mechanisms, or by cognitive processes—learn to utilize them in looking at his own temporal experience.

8. The stage may thus be set for reorganization or, in the language of experimentalists, for recoding of time experience.

Despite the use of the word *coding*, however, the following brief clinical illustration deals with "time feeling" rather than with even a subjective "time image"—in analogy to the distinction between Federn's "bodily ego feeling" (1952) and Schilder's "body image" (1950). The analyst's sensitivity to the patient's changing experiences of duration can facilitate clinical work because of the intimate connection of subjective time experience and affective life.

Mr. Brown, a professional man who had been raised by adoptive parents, lived alternately with his mistress and his wife during the course of his analysis. In one analytic session, when he had been living for a prolonged period with his wife, he spoke of his feeling of progress in his analytic work but also spoke at length of his difficulty in "seeing himself" during his most recent prolonged period with his mistress, which had terminated almost two years previously. After the analyst commented that he had seemed more different from hour to hour during that period than he did now, the patient gradually began to describe his feeling that periods spent with his mistress had a different time texture from periods spent with his wife and children. Although his description of people, situations, and feelings was complex, his focus was on the struggle to reexperience and reintegrate his time-out, his discontinuity of experience, his effort to "see" himself both in more constant times and in saccadic periods of rapid mood changes. He then talked about the eventual termination of the analysis, his anticipated joyful and nostalgic feelings. This was followed by talk of his plans to ask his adoptive parents about his biologic parents, whom he believed they knew. Historical details that he had never mentioned before about his adoptive parents began to come out, and fantasies about his biologic parents as well. He then said that there might be a connection between characteristics of his mistress and of his fantasied parents. In the next session, in the context of expressing fears about what he might discover concerning his origins and how he would react to the discoveries—and in the context of talking about plans, wishes, and fears for his future—he reported a dream of being in a corner room from which one could see in two directions.

Connecting events and feelings differently—in a sense, therefore, bringing new information to bear on episodes reexperienced during psychoanalysis—permits a reorganization and reinterpretation of time feeling. Experiments dealing with the effects of new information on time experience may be somewhat analogous to this aspect of clinical development. In a metaphorical representation of the process, I visualize a rod traversing many layers of fluid with different angles of refraction; the psychoanalytic restructuring functions as if it were stirring up and intermixing these layers. In that way, the treatment may enhance the patient's sense of continuity and facilitate the widening and future extension of temporal perspective.

Temporal Perspective

I have addressed the problem of temporal perspective in work on the clinical use of autobiographical projections into the future, or "future autobiographies" (Kafka and Bolgar, 1949). We modified a technique used by Israeli (1936) so as to adapt it for use as a projective technique for veterans—psychiatric patients who had previously been exposed to so much testing that diminishing returns had set in when conventional evaluative procedures were used. When it became important to evaluate the clinical status of such test-sophisticated and test-weary individuals, we asked them to make future projections, using the following instructions: "This is a day in [five years hence]. Describe the course of your day."

After the task was completed, we asked our patients to again place themselves five years in the future and list the major events of their lives going backward from that future date. With this second step we wanted to investigate whether or not there was a continuity from imagined future through actual past in such a projected retrospective view. In my refraction metaphor, one can visualize the rod as traversing fluid layers representing future, present, and past. If the layers have fixed viscosities and are not intermixed, differential refraction will produce apparent angles in the rod, whereas a degree of mixing or amalgamation will make the rod appear straight. If affective components differentially alter *reality testing* of future projection, current experience, and memories of the past, these different "viscosities" will be revealed. The second step in the procedure thus supplemented the information obtained in the first.

Our patients were given the two instructions of the future autobiography (FA) procedure in a face-to-face situation, and there was some pressure to respond rapidly. Under these circumstances it became clear that at first wishes and/or fears were prominent. The shift to an assessment of what was realistically possible or likely was impossible for some, difficult for others, and less difficult for still others; the difficulty varied in different areas of life—for instance, in work, marriage, and parenting. We found it convenient to use the following three points of reference:

1. To what extent is the future structured?
2. To what extent are reality factors taken into consideration?
3. What is the specific content and what are the significant emphases and/or omissions of the FA?

Light was thrown on point 1 primarily by the difficulty the subject had in performing the tasks. The degree of difficulty was reflected by the subject's productivity, the variety of content, comments about the task, hesitations, blushing, perspiring, and sometimes discrepancies in content in the two forms of the FA.

Occasionally a subject finds it almost impossible even to grasp the idea of future. One severely depressed patient misunderstood the instructions repeatedly and proceeded to write about events five years before rather than five years hence. In general we confirmed the frequently reported observation that turning toward the future is an especially difficult task for depressed subjects. We also noted a constriction of the temporal field, both future and past, in some patients with recent traumatic experiences.

Information on point 2, the consideration of reality factors, came mostly from the clinician's evaluation of the FA in the light of all other information about the subject. When, for instance, an adult subject with meager educational background and rather modest intellectual endowment saw himself as studying brain surgery five years hence, we thought we were justified in speaking of some disregard of reality factors.

The approach to the content analysis—point 3—was not essentially different from that used in the analysis of other projective material. The relative amounts of detail employed to describe different elements of the subject's future life were especially noteworthy. A single young woman, for example, gave a detailed description of her future son, including his behavior, his name, and his face, voice, and hair color. The only specific mention of a husband, however, occurred in the following sentence: "My husband is in the bathroom already, and now I am making breakfast, listening to my son's early morning discoveries, and seeing if he is getting dressed for nursery school."

In some FAs all people are anonymous, but in some that are rich in detail and full of real people, it is interesting to note the devices used by subjects to avoid facing those living people and some of the problems associated with them. Displacement of emphasis is perhaps the most subtle and flexible of such devices. It is as if unstructured, confused areas, holes, or blank faces were left in the otherwise well-completed structure of the individual's future. Murray (1938) has expressed well the relationship between the "enduring purpose" and the resolved conflict. The less the conflicts are resolved, the less one should expect synthesis and creative integration in future autobiographies. In any such procedure, the areas, or "themas," as Murray called them, that are the least integrated—that is, in which enduring purposes are relatively absent—can be expected to be related to unresolved conflicts. In our work with the FA, anxiety and evasion, but also extremely optimistic statements—especially when the subject could not justify his optimism—pointed toward such unresolved conflicts. When a subject described in his FA how good he felt (five years in the future) about one area in his life (for example, his work) without giving any details about it, invariably we found that this area represented a most severe problem at the present time.

The depressed subject mentioned above who repeatedly misunderstood the instruction finally wrote, "I feel as though everything is going fine and I have made something of my life. I like the new position." But he was unable to say what the new position would be and was only able to specify, "I would come in regular dress clothes—not working clothes—wouldn't be real tired out." He spontaneously added later, "I'm afraid that I won't be able to make a living. In five years I'll be ten times as bad as I am now."

In general our observations led us to formulate the following hypotheses:

1. The early reaction to an invitation to formulate a FA is a strongly affective one (either hope or dread).

2. The speed with which the shift to a reasonably realistic description of the future can be accomplished is a function of at least three factors: (a) the relative lack of important unresolved conflicts, (b) the effective functioning level of immediate defenses, and (c) the subject's intelligence.

Toward the end of our study we began to compare the future autobiographies of husbands and wives. Although we did not pursue this procedure systematically, it immediately became apparent that the technique could bring into sharp focus areas of conflict and areas of congruence of expectations. The technique also highlighted differences and similarities in the reality-testing functions of the two spouses.

Although this look at the marital dyad dealt specifically with future perspective, it can illuminate many other time-related matters that are also strikingly important in the psychotherapeutic or psychoanalytic dyad. Among them are the effects of transference developments on interpersonal timing and on temporal disorientation and the confusing sensations when an analytic session seems endless to the analyst and short to the patient, or vice versa. When the termination phase approaches, however, not only is the analysand in touch with his own range of available temporal graining but analyst and analysand also have a subtle mutual understanding of such graining, of the temporal perspective in which it is placed, and of how temporal perspective is reexperienced in a telescoped form in an individual hour. Jaffe (1971) has described how his patient perceived a reconstruction in a series of the analyst's interpretations—in effect, an indication that the analyst anticipated termination, for which the patient said she was not quite ready.

The individual's personal temporal graining, the patterns and textures of the grids that are available to him, organizes the flow of his experiences into object constancies in at least one sense. To the extent, therefore, that the analyst is responsive to his patient's multiple ways of graining experience of time, he is responsive to his patient's multiple realities (Kafka, 1964). Acquaintance and reacquaintance with the possibilities of shared rhythms of organizing experience contribute to the analysand's exploration and development of individual variations of common rhythms and realities. Perhaps some congruence between the analyst's and the patient's future perspectives, at least in terms of the *possibilities* of the analysand's future, is also achieved at this point.

Thus, in the study of temporal experience, the clinician and the experimenter discover that their findings are applicable to each other's world. I will develop the concept of *temporal graining of realities* at greater length after other theoretical, experimental, and clinical aspects of the encompassing concept of *multiple realities* have been examined more closely.

Chapter 2

Thinking and the Constant Objects: The Double Bind Upended

In everyday usage people tend to speak as if there were one universally recognized commonsense reality. But at the same time most of us are aware not only that different individuals have different perceptions of reality but also that our own perception of reality can change with the passage of time and in varying environments. Modern physical science has gone further in recognizing such variable perceptions and has found the idea of a commonsense reality inadequate to its tasks, as illustrated by the realities dealt with by quantum and wave theory. In the field of psychiatry and psychoanalysis, the limitations of the concept of one commonsense reality are so striking that therapists must approach the problems emerging from their encounter with multiple realities from every available direction. Although I will emphasize the practical clinical and technical applications of a concept of multiple realities, the formal logical considerations cannot be ignored.

The psychiatric patient's psychological reality at any one moment is a particular pattern of organization of stimuli, and such patterns are in constant flux. Nevertheless, psychiatrists and psychoanalysts apply a concept of reality testing in which the reality is the commonsense reality of stable objects, of objects and people with a considerable degree of rigid identity. Although this identity is a building block of common sense, psychiatrists—using their own common sense—are constantly faced with the problem of comprehending the apparent lack of a sense of rigid identity in their patients.

In approaching this problem, *comprehending*, or *encompassing*, should be differentiated from *understanding*. We may learn to understand a mathematical formula containing the negative of a square root, but most of us, most of the time, will not be able to comprehend it.[1] To comprehend, or encompass, something means that it becomes part of our experience. This means that we must feel it, but it cannot be the total of our felt experience. We must grasp it by means of something that is bigger than the object to be grasped. To comprehend, encompass, the problem of identity in psychiatry—the identity of the self, the identity of other persons, and the identity of objects—we must use a conceptual tool that is wider than the concept of identity. Even to describe the development of a reality based on some constancy, we need a concept dealing with the organization of stimuli, a concept that does not take identity for granted.

Artiss (1962, p. 140) and Arieti (1963) are among the authors who have dealt with this problem. Artiss describes how the child permits his parents to define reality for him by granting them the "naming prerogative." To present this concept, Artiss uses the device of a hypothetical argument between parent and child. The child questions the authority of the parents to give him a name. If the child refused to grant his parents the prerogative to name him John Doe, he would, for instance, be able to say, "I'm Jesus," and then the "schizophrenic analogue would have already appeared." Although designed to illustrate identity formation, Artiss's hypo-

1. It is my private belief, which is not essential to the theme being developed here, that the march of science is from understanding to comprehending. This belief is related to the observation that theoretically derived mathematical formulae often soon find practical scientific applications in the world of experience. My belief may also be related to the great interest that some schizophrenic patients show in new scientific developments. For example, for some delusional patients who see themselves as observed from a distance, the invention of television has served as a kind of proof that they are not so crazy after all. I also believe that each new scientific invention may induce hope in some patients that their "wider reality" will be less derogated.

thetical argument between parents and child is a formal device particularly dependent on the rigid identity of words precisely because it is an argument. In an example from my own experience, Mary, an adult patient who literally struggled with the problem of the naming prerogative, had had severe generalized dermatitis during the language-learning period, which had hampered the integration of language with body experience (this patient will be discussed in more detail later). The conceptual framework I am developing here, building on such examples, uses the fluidity of perception more than the rigid identity of the word.

Arieti, in discussing schizophrenic thought processes, quotes Von Domarus's principle, which states: "Whereas the normal person accepts identity only upon the basis of identical subjects, the schizophrenic may accept identity based on identical predicates." Arieti writes, "If . . . a schizophrenic happens to think, 'The Virgin Mary was a virgin, I am a virgin,' she may conclude 'I am the Virgin Mary.' . . . For normal persons a class is a collection of objects to which a concept applies. . . . In paleological thinking . . . a class is a collection of objects which have a predicate or part in common" (p. 59). Arieti, however, fails to point out in this context that what is part and what is whole, what is subject and what is predicate, are not building blocks of experience but are themselves the results of experience. When a patient has experienced a *characteristic* of a person as being more fundamental, more lasting, more "identical," than the person as a whole, this characteristic acquires qualities of the *subject*, and the person, then merely a personification of the more stable idea, acquires qualities of the *predicate*.

For example, Dorothy L., a highly intelligent schizophrenic patient (also to be discussed later) who was in remission, told me that during her recent psychotic episode a nurse with a foreign accent and blonde hair had seemed to her to be the literary character Heidi. After many years of work with me, the patient was able to communicate that because she had loved the book *Heidi*, Heidi-like characteristics were much more important and more stable to her than a person's identity as a whole. She experienced neither herself nor anyone else as having any continuity of existence, any identity as a person, at that time. The idea or feeling of "Heidi-ness" did have some continuity. What is subject here and what is predicate? Such accounts have led me to think that a technically more useful term than "feeling of identity" is "subjective equivalence over a period of time." "Subjective equivalence" refers to Heinrich Klüver's "method of equivalent stimuli" (1933).

Klüver observed that the increasing refinement of experiments in comparative psychology led to the decreasing psychological significance of the findings. A traditional approach in comparative psychology would be to study the smallest difference between two stimuli to which an organism can respond. What is the smallest difference in grayness, for instance, that the animal can perceive? Klüver felt that the more experiments of this kind were freed from "interfering" factors, the more they approached physiological experiments, perhaps ultimately the study of the biochemistry of the end organs. When experimental refinement reduced the significance of the findings, Klüver then thought it would be more meaningful to study how *great* the difference between stimuli could be before the animal would fail to recognize similarities. Let us say, for example, that an animal is trained to jump for food and to select the square when confronted with a large black square and a small red circle, both on a white background. If we now present the animal with the same foreground figures on a blue background, will he still jump for food and select the square? Is the situation subjectively equivalent? The answer cannot be taken for granted, but if it is affirmative, we might further complicate the situation by confronting the animal with the red circle and a large black oval instead of a square. In that way we could test the range of subjectively equivalent stimuli for the animal trained originally to jump in response to a large black square on a white ground.

It can easily be seen that on the one hand this kind of experiment is related to tests of abstract reasoning, and that on the other it is related to the problem of object constancy, as the term is used in general psychology. As I shall demonstrate, it also contributes to the psychoanalytic meaning of the concept. In general psychology, object constancy refers to the phenomenon whereby a table, say, seen from different angles, with their different retinal images, remains the same table for a normal person. Subjective equivalence is thus related to the identity of the objects. The patterns of

subjective equivalence for any person are, of course, largely determined by emotional and motivational factors. It is thus concep-
tually possible that at a particular time I will see my neighbor as
more subjectively equivalent to my current self-perception than
my own memory of how I was yesterday. In such a situation, one
can talk of identity fusion with the neighbor. For anyone working
with psychotic patients, these are not far-fetched conceptualizations. In the context of these considerations, a feeling of identity
can be described in terms of the experience of subjective equivalence of ego states over a period of time. (I am here referring to ego
states as though we were dealing with particulate units, in a sense
"quanta," and not, in this context, as transitional "wave" phenomena.) The concept of subjective equivalence is not foreign to
the usual frame of reference in dynamic psychiatry. For example,
the coalescence of "the good mother" and "the bad mother" into
"mother" might be regarded as the establishment of a subjective
equivalence. The concept can also be applied to the idea of "transference."

To summarize thus far: commonsense reality and commonsense logic, which have limits in everyday life and are inadequate
in physical science, are even more inadequate in psychiatry. Commonsense logic is based on the principle of identity. We cannot
"comprehend" the concept of the feeling of identity using a
conceptual tool smaller than, not encompassing, what is to be
"grasped." Psychological reality for a person at any one time is a
pattern of organization of stimuli and can be described in terms of
a pattern of subjective equivalences. The advantages of this descriptive concept are twofold. First, subjective equivalence is an
operational concept that permits a bridge from psychiatry to other
behavioral sciences. It leaves room for information obtained by
the usual psychodynamic approaches—such as the fusion of
"good" and "bad" mother into "mother." But the pattern of
equivalences can be studied in terms of many theoretical approaches, such as imprinting, conditioning, the views of Piaget,
and so forth. Second, the concept has a wide scope of applicability,
ranging from problems of abstract thinking to those of subjective
identity and object constancy. It thus allows a rational approach to
the paradoxical thoughts and contradictory perceptions that are

often present in moments of therapeutic significance (as I shall demonstrate with clinical examples).

Although no one pattern of subjective equivalences is in and of itself any more valid, true, or real than any other pattern (just as Euclidean geometry is no more valid than any other geometry), the parents of the nonpsychotic child have succeeded in giving more weight to one pattern of subjective equivalences than to the multiplicity of other possible patterns. A solid anchor in one reality coexisting with an ability to encompass many realities, even paradoxical patterns of subjective equivalences, could be described in terms of the ability to "regress in the service of the ego."[2]

Let us now consider the implications for work in psychiatry of such a relativistic view of psychological reality. Much attention has been paid to the psychiatrist's culturally determined value system and the effects of his value orientation on his work. The values generally considered are in the traditional area of ethics; routine value judgment in favor of "commonsense-identity logic" is not made explicit. But patients are as sensitive to value judgments concerning formal aspects of their thought as they are to derogatory value judgments concerning their feelings and aspirations. As I indicated, specific technical applications of the concepts refer to the place of paradox in psychotherapy and therapeutic management. The recognition that some significant therapeutic steps involve, in *retrospect*, a paradox should not be mistaken for advocacy of contrived irrationality. I might here compare the therapist in the treatment situation to the chief of a clan or a head of state. Just as a clan chief or national leader often holds his position because more realities are acceptable to him than to those he leads, the therapist can be of help to the patient because of his wider perspective on possible realities.

The idea of wider reality is implicitly present in the classical psychoanalytic attitude of free-floating attention. The history of psychotherapeutic approaches to psychotic patients shares an evo-

2. It could also be discussed in terms of the child's acceptance of contradiction, as opposed to his malignant vulnerability to a double-bind situation, in which he reacts to contradictory injunctions by denying their existence. I believe that this denial of contradiction changes the mere expression of ambivalence into a true double bind. I shall say more about this later.

lution from a narrower to a wider stance. Paul Federn advocated different therapists for the same patient in the regressed and compensated phases of his illness (1952). My conversations with several clinicians who have worked with Frieda Fromm-Reichmann revealed that her interest in id contacts between therapist and psychotic patient changed to an emphasis on ego contacts, contact with the intact or mature areas. More recent developments in psychoanalytically oriented treatment centers, conceptualized only in retrospect, show a gradual diminution of such "either-or" attitudes. The therapist who may have joined the patient in deeply regressive material in one hour may the same day participate with the same patient in a matter-of-fact discussion about the work program in an all-hospital meeting. In a dynamically oriented hospital, a therapist may even see a patient in a wet-sheet pack on one day and invite him to a meal outside the hospital the next day. The therapist's ability to reject stereotyped notions about incongruity may be a potent therapeutic factor.

The following are examples of shifts in experienced reality—examples of apparently paradoxical situations, collected in work with hospitalized patients.

A woman who had made considerable social improvement requested a change to outpatient status. The request was refused because the social improvement was interpreted as a calculated façade and because such a move might be utilized as a distancing maneuver. The patient pointed out that her ability to *calculate* her behavior was, after her wildly psychotic period, a sign of improvement that should lead to outpatient status. The therapist recognized the existence of a paradox but did not change his position. The same patient soon thereafter made a perceptive report to the administrator about happenings on the ward during the weekend. Upon hearing the report, a nurse said to the administrator, "Why don't you make her a staff member?" The administrator thought the suggestion had merit, and the possibility was seriously considered that a patient for whom outpatient status had just been refused should be paid to work as an aide in the *patient* work program. This represents, I believe, a true shift in reality. At the moment when the administrator agreed to give the patient a job as an aide, he perceived her, and she perceived herself, in a different "reality." The patient's experience should not be confused with Alexander's "corrective emotional experience," which is based on conscious role playing. The notions developed here may be useful in conceptualizing the multiplicity of roles in any hospital program in which patients not only help other patients but may even assume positions of responsibility for each other (Kafka, 1964).

In another example of the retrospective shift, Mary had for years used self-mutilation as a blackmail technique. After one of several symptom-free periods, she requested outpatient status because, she said, continued living with disturbed patients might lead to recurrence of her symptom. The therapist supported the patient's request, but the administrator said, "No, it's the same old blackmail." The reality, however, had changed: the therapist, who recognized the patient's new self-perception, no longer saw such a request as blackmail.

The last example supplies a developmental analogy: when a mother permits her baby to take the first step, she does not "overcome her fear," she does not "accept the possibility" of the baby's fall. Rather, for a moment the reality for mother and baby must be that he is not going to fall, a wider reality that to the bystander looks like a delusion or a folie à deux. We are here, I believe, dealing with the primary paradox of individuation, the symbiosis that permits the child to step away from its mother, when love and mutual acceptance of separateness become subjectively equivalent.

Multiple Reality and Double-Bind Theory

Being anchored in one reality while retaining the ability to encompass many reality organizations is obviously related to the problems of interest to double-bind theorists. In contrast to such theorists, who have argued that exposures to multiple and contradictory injunctions or realities tend to be pathogenic, I have been impressed by the positive, "healthy" aspects of the ability to tolerate different reality organizations. Nevertheless, double-bind theory seemed a promising approach to difficult problems. In 1964 I was consultant to a project at the National Institute of Mental Health in which characteristics of newlywed or about-to-be-wed couples were being studied. The study was *prospective* in that it assessed the potential influence of characteristics of the couples on such future traits of their children as psychological health and the nature of pathology. Before beginning the study, we asked ourselves what characteristics of the prospective parents should be investigated in a project designed to circumvent the usual vicissitudes of retrospective genetic reconstructions. We concluded that a hypothesis and research design based on *formal* characteristics of communication patterns would be easier to manage than a hypothesis deriving from the infinite number of possible kinds of content. Double-bind theory offered such a formal hypothesis and seemed to deserve closer scrutiny.

The paradoxical communication that is a primary element of double-bind theory is related to the more general topic of ambiguity. A number of separate clinical and theoretical projects can be profitably considered under the heading of ambiguity, especially its positive aspects—that is, the significance of the hunger for and tolerance of ambiguity. The formal definition of ambiguity can help us understand its implications and the nature of paradoxical communication. Although in everyday language, information is often said to be ambiguous when it is conflictual, in the language of formal logic, information is ambiguous only when the conflicting data are of different "logical types"—that is, are on different levels of abstraction. Formally, ambiguity is an abbreviation of the expression "ambiguity of types" or—more completely—"ambiguity of logical types." A *paradoxical* communication can always be shown to consist of conflicting data that are on different levels of abstraction. Although psychologically we associate ambiguity with uncertainty more than with paradox, ambiguous and paradoxical communications are logically synonymous.

The aspects of double-bind theory that have been best developed formally emphasize that *overexposure* to paradoxical communication is pathogenic or, more specifically, schizophrenogenic. Since my own clinical observation suggested that the unavoidable exposure to ambiguous situations in daily life was less tolerable, more "dissociative," and more "uncanny" for those who had early *underexposure* to paradoxical communications, I found myself in apparent opposition to the main tenet of double-bind theory. Furthermore, underexposure of the offspring to ambiguity during crucial developmental phases seemed related to parental fear of paradox. Although double-bind theorists also refer to "therapeutic double binds," those are *formally* similar to the pathogenic variety. They are described as occurring in a more benevolent interpersonal atmosphere, but their formal similarity creates conceptual difficulties that constitute an obstacle to the research application of the theory.

If it had indeed been possible to identify pathogenic double-bind communications on the basis of formal characteristics alone, it would have been relatively easy to locate young parents who have a tendency to communicate in this fashion, and their offspring could have been contrasted later with those of parents not prone to issue such double-bind messages. Difficulties encountered in other objective studies using the double-bind concept have been reviewed by Olson (1969). Our own difficulties in identifying "pathogenic double-binders" were related to (1) the problem of discriminating between benevolent, "therapeutic" binds and pathogenic binds, (2) the ubiquity of paradox (for instance, wives asking husbands to be spontaneously more affectionate [Ryder 1970]), (3) the observation that in human communication the level of abstraction is in constant flux, and (4) the finding that shifts in levels of abstraction could probably not be differentiated from shifts in role relationship. Double-bind theory thus was not directly useful for the intended research design. Nevertheless, the analysis of the difficulties and a critical examination of the theory contributed to a reformulation of ideas concerning paradoxical parental communication.

Critical Evaluation of Double-Bind Theory

Double-bind theory states that a history of exposure to inescapable communication traps is schizophrenogenic, and it attempts to explain the patient's feeling of being trapped, an experience to which the therapist has easy empathic access. Bateson et al. (1956) give recognizable examples, such as that of a young man who had fairly well recovered from an acute schizophrenic episode and was visited in the hospital by his mother. Glad to see her, he impulsively put his arm around her shoulders, but she stiffened. When he withdrew his arm, she asked, "Don't you love me any more?" In response he blushed, at which point she told him not to be so easily embarrassed and afraid of his feelings. The patient had received the messages that he must and that he must not show his affection to his mother in order to keep his ties with her. Impressed by and sensitized to such impossible, no-win situations, the clinician seems to encounter them everywhere. The father of Susan, a schizophrenic girl, for instance, had made major changes in his career as a clergyman in order to pay for her treatment in a private hospital. Despite a recent heart attack, he had left his pulpit and had become a hard-driving, nationally prominent lecturer and author. During a visit to the hospital he explained both to his daughter and to the staff that he owed his newfound energy, the renewal in his life, to the financial needs of her expensive hospitalization. One could say, on the basis of these data, that the patient was caught in a double bind. If she made successful efforts to recover rapidly, she might deprive her father of the reported source of renewal in his life. If she failed to improve sufficiently to be discharged from the hospital, the associated financial need might impose a "killing" work load on father. On the face of it, she was in a no-win situation.

A similar trap apparently characterized the following case. Bernard, the musically talented son of a conductor, had received communications from his family throughout his early life to the effect that the only truly valuable lifetime activity was to be a musician. At the same time he had been told again and again about tragedies associated with sons of musicians who had attempted to follow in their fathers' footsteps. He was told that in such a situation, the competitive effort was destructive not only to the son but also to the family name, to the father's name. Despite his fervently expressed wish for musical training, it was withheld from him in the musically saturated household. At the age of six or seven, he developed a peculiar mannerism of running to his father, making a "staccato" contact, briefly throwing his arms around him, and then running away from him as fast as he could. Prominent features of the clinical picture were extreme vacillation from notions of grandeur to feelings of abject worthlessness, a fractionation of self-representation, and a general ideational lack of continuity.

I will later amplify this and other case material, but for now these examples show that the "damned if you do, damned if you don't" situation described by double-bind theory offers a seductively elegant and immediately plausible framework in which to place clinical observations. As an example of a therapeutic double bind, Bateson et al. cited an episode from a case treated by Frieda Fromm-Reichmann (later fictionalized in *I Never Promised You a Rose Garden* by "Hannah Green"). At one point the patient informed the therapist of her delusional god. The therapist responded that she did not believe in this god and then instructed the patient to ask her delusional god for permission to work in therapy with the doctor. The therapist thus had her patient in a therapeutic double bind. If the patient was made to doubt the existence of her god, then she would be agreeing with Fromm-Reichmann and admitting her attachment to therapy. If she insisted that the god was real and asked his permission to work in therapy, then she would be implying that Fromm-Reichmann was "more powerful" than he—again admitting her involvement with the therapist.

Like the pathogenic double bind, the therapeutic one is formed by conflicting information involving a shift in the level of abstraction. As I indicated above, the similarity of the formally defined features of therapeutic and pathogenic binds greatly complicates attempts to identify them differentially for research purposes in the study of actual communication sequences. This is especially true *if one conceives of and looks for paradoxes that may "promote individuation"* —and in this sense could perhaps be called therapeutic—*in nontherapy situations.* Bateson and his coworkers, however, focus on the role they ascribe to the double bind in the etiology of schizophrenia when they indicate the necessary ingredients for a double-bind situation: (1) two or more persons, (2) repeated experience, (3) a primary negative injunction, (4) a secondary injunction conflicting with the first *at a more abstract level* and, like the first, enforced by punishment or signals that threaten survival, and (5) a tertiary negative injunction prohibiting the victim from escaping from the field.

What most specifically, pointedly, and interestingly distinguishes this from other conflict theories is the focus on the shift in the level of abstraction. Such qualitatively different conflicts are paradoxes. How does a paradox, a term synonymous with "ambiguity of type," differ from a contradiction? Watzlawick et al. (1967) illustrate a contradiction by a stop sign to which is nailed another sign reading "no stopping at any time." In this *contradictory* situation one has the *choice* of obeying one or the other of the two injunctions. Correspondingly, if a father tells his son not to tattletale and also asks him how his younger sister got into trouble, the father is making *contradictory* requests. Presumably, the son can *choose* which injunction to obey. The role relationship between father and son in the context of the "no tattletale" injunction, however, is different from their role relationship in the context of the request for information about the sister. The latter request may carry the implication "Son, in this particular situation, you are seen as more like an adult, like me, and you should help me protect and educate a child." Questions of such possible shifts in levels of abstraction raise doubts about the existence of "pure" contradictions in ordinary communication. This is another factor complicating the identification of paradoxes, as opposed to contradictions, when communication sequences are analyzed for research purposes.

Watzlawick et al. formally illustrate a paradox by a photograph of an overpass spanning a roadbed. On the overpass is a sign saying, "Ignore this sign." This sign, presumably a practical joke, is formally not contradictory, but it creates a true paradox through its self-reflexivity. In order to ignore it, one must notice it. But the very act of noticing it disobeys the injunction itself. Therefore, the sign can be obeyed only through disobedience. The nature of such paradoxes was studied by Whitehead and Russell (1910). Russell's theory of types observes that paradoxes involve different levels of abstraction that are not immediately apparent. The "Ignore this sign" paradox, for instance, contains such a hidden shift since the *word* "sign" and the *material sign* on which the word is written involve different levels of abstraction. Whitehead and Russell would say that in the preceding sentence I have made explicit the hidden shift in "logical types"—I have communicated about the paradoxical communication; that is, I have "metacommunicated" and have thus *escaped* the paradox. This aspect of a formal logical approach to paradoxes is relevant to double-bind theory, which postulates that someone who is inundated by paradoxical parental communications, coupled with taboos against "metacommunicating," is at greater risk for schizophrenia. Another aspect of Whitehead and Russell's work is even more congruent with the reformulation I am proposing, as I shall demonstrate.

Reformulation of Ideas on Parental Paradoxical Communication: Formal Basis

My reformulation focuses on the effects of relative parental *avoidance* of expression of paradox and of poor parental tolerance of ambiguity. These effects are experiences of *dissonance* for the developing offspring, who inevitably is confronted by other experiential data that are ambiguous and full of paradox and that somehow have to be included in his "reality." In contrast, parental *tolerance* of the irreconcilable paradoxes that the child must encounter in his educational and playful exploration of his expanding world help him to cope with those paradoxes. The parents' casual reactions to phenomena that everyone is compelled both to notice and not to notice can help with the child's gradual integration of parental realities and his own evolving formulations of realities. Such integration also helps the child relate to his parents as positive objects, in the psychoanalytic sense of the word, at the same time that it makes possible a necessary degree of accommodation to the paradoxical systems that are to represent reality.

Although this thesis is primarily derived from and will be supported by clinical observations, the following brief additional excursion into modern formal logic reveals forcefully a congruent theme.

Bateson et al. focused on Russell's techniques for *escaping* paradoxes, but Whitehead and Russell recommend the use of their escape technique only *after* one has been caught in a trap. They specifically warn, however, against too much caution about avoiding traps. They point out that reasoning would have to come to a standstill if rigorous attempts were made to avoid the *possibility* of paradox even in the most formal logical chain. Specifically, they talk of the *necessity* of ambiguity of types in order to make a chain of reasoning apply to any of an infinite number of cases, which would not be possible if one were to avoid using typically ambiguous words and symbols. Thus, even the classical syllogism contains some "ambiguity of types." For example, let us consider the syllogism "All men are mortal. Socrates is a man. Therefore, Socrates is mortal." Not quite so, Russell would say: we do not know that Socrates is mortal until he is dead.

In arguing for the necessity for ambiguity, Whitehead and Russell do not present formal proofs. Kurt Gödel (1931), however, has gone beyond them by proving *formally* the necessary incompleteness of a finite system. What Gödel formally proved is that "if arithmetic is consistent, its consistency cannot be established by metamathematical reasoning that can be represented within the formalism of arithmetic" (Nagel and Newman, 1958, p. 7).

Nagel and Newman, who have made Gödel's work accessible to the nonmathematician, point out that his argument does not eliminate the possibility of strictly finitistic proofs that cannot be represented within arithmetic (p. 98). But no one today appears to have a clear idea of what a finitistic proof that is not capable of formulation within arithmetic would be like. What is significant about Gödel's work in connection with my proposed reformulation is his demonstration that one has to jump to ever more inclusive levels of abstraction even in formal logical procedures in order to avoid triviality. He thus offers formal support to Whitehead and Russell's more impressionistic warning *not* to avoid the possibility of paradoxes. This is congruent with a clinically based reformulation emphasizing the psychological necessity of appropriate exposure to ambiguity. Gödel's demonstration may also facilitate a sharpening of conceptual focus in this reformulation: the developing individual, who must operate in an *open* system, experiences dissonance for which he has not been prepared when his parents operate and communicate as though a *closed* system were the only one in existence.

While self-consistency in a closed system is associated with triviality in modern logic, analogous reduction to one level of abstraction, in operational terms, is unthinkable in living systems, especially in human experience and communication. The study of our very perceptual process bolsters the idea I presented in the introduction—that with each perception we pass rapidly through various stages and levels of organization. I will later discuss in some detail the tachistoscopic presentation of Rorschach cards (Stein, 1949), which shows that in reacting to such a display we recapitulate our perceptual history. For now, I want to underline that the briefest tachistoscopic exposures result in the most "concrete" responses, resembling those of a child, and longer exposures involve higher levels of abstraction, adult responses.

Thus, as I hinted earlier, a rigorous distinction between contradiction, which involves one level of abstraction, and paradox, which involves more than one level, cannot meaningfully be applied to ordinary human interchanges. A conversation, words spoken and heard, any living communication, can be placed in more than one level of abstraction. Strictly speaking, *any* contradiction is a paradox, but what creates a sharp paradoxical experience—as with the "ignore this sign" sign—is the degree of unpreparedness for the nature of the shift in the levels of abstraction involved.[3]

Psychological "reality" depends on our abstracting level of the moment. Earlier in this chapter, I referred to Klüver's (1933, 1936) study of how great the differences between stimuli can be before a subject fails to recognize similarities. His method determines the limits of *the levels of abstraction* within which there is still *subjective equivalence*. I emphasized that such patterns of subjective equivalence—the patterns of organization, of abstraction—are the very building blocks of our realities, of our patterns

3. Certain transitional periods, such as courtship and early marriage, involve considerable shifts—for which one may be poorly prepared—in role relationships and in the levels of abstraction that have to be bridged. If the magnitude of the shifts makes it necessary, semiritualized intervention of third parties permits bride and groom to have a discontinuity of experience before they are presented with a "new reality." Some social factors that help bridge experiences of discontinuity have been considered in "Separating and Joining Influences in Courtship and Early Marriage" (Ryder et al., 1971). In a later chapter the place of rituals in shifts in *role* and in levels of abstraction, and the connection between these shifts, will be more fully explored.

of object constancy, as the term is used in both experimental psychological *and* psychoanalytic literature. If one individual's "reality possibilities" are thus tied to the range of his levels of abstraction, his communication to another depends on some degree of correspondence between his and the other's range of levels of abstraction. In chapter 1, I discussed the timing in ordinary conversation. It is our judgment of the level of abstraction to which any partner in a conversation will carry our words that largely influences this timing (Kafka, 1957b). Searles's (1965) clinical descriptions of disorienting, "crazy"-making patterns of communication imply veritable acrobatics in shifts of levels of abstraction.

We are prepared for some of the distances that can exist between levels of abstraction but not for others. The differences between these kinds of distances are *objectively quantitative*, but they lead to experiences that differ in *subjectively qualitative* ways. Psychologically, shifts in abstraction level for which we are prepared are associated with experiences we may continue to call contradictions; shifts for which we are not prepared are associated with experiences we may continue to call paradoxes. The former are related to *ambivalence* and the latter to a somewhat *uncanny* feeling, a mild form of which we experience when we think of ourselves as trapped (when in a mood in which we cannot quite laugh it off), as by the "ignore this sign" sign.

My use of the terms *ambiguity* and *paradox* in further clinical discussions will reflect these considerations. Mary, the self-mutilator, for instance, who cuts herself to find out whether or not she is alive, is trying to escape from *ambiguity* and not from a simple contradiction, since the distance between the levels of abstraction involved in experiencing "aliveness" and "deadness" is not one for which she is at that moment prepared. I will explore the ambiguity of aliveness and deadness, and its connection to the animate and the inanimate, more thoroughly later.

Reformulation: Clinical Basis

My interest in paradoxical communications and the observation that they were ubiquitous ultimately led me to question their schizophrenogenic role, even in the light of qualifications specified by double-bind theory for their pathogenicity (Kafka, 1971b). In a later chapter, I will deal more systematically with schizophrenic thought disorder, but some comments on related factors are appropriate in the present context.

As I mentioned earlier, on closer analysis of double-bind data, I gained the impression, in opposition to the theory, that there might be a relative *paucity* of ambiguous expression in some families of schizophrenic patients. Ringuette and Kennedy (1966) found that a group of double-bind experts—that is, individuals who had been involved in the development and formulation of the double-bind concept—had a poor interjudge reliability in identifying double binds in letters written by mothers of schizophrenic patients. In my experience, when clinicians tend to agree on the existence of a double bind, they are referring to situations in which patients, and more typically parents of patients, have made striking and bizarre defensive maneuvers when confronted with the paradoxes they had expressed. Compared to random clinical material, the paradoxes themselves are often not particularly unusual; it is the response to confrontation that forces the issue into the therapist's awareness. The letters in the Ringuette and Kennedy study do not permit the clinician to observe such responses to confrontation with paradoxes.

In the example, cited earlier, of the clergyman who communicated to his hospitalized daughter, Susan, and to the staff that her expensive hospitalization was forcing him to adopt a "never more happy" life-style and a pace that was also "killing him," the paradox itself was not so unusual. But the response to confrontation with the paradox—which involved the issue of the clergyman's life or death on one level of abstraction and the quality of his life on another level—was notable. In a late-afternoon interview, the family consultant at the hospital made an initial attempt to play back to the father the no-win situation in which his communication was apparently placing his daughter. An appointment was made to explore the matter further the next morning. When the family consultant arrived for the interview, he was given a message saying that the father had unexpectedly had to join his other daughter, who lived in another city, because she had telephoned him about a sudden disturbed and involved relationship with her psychiatrist. Shortly thereafter the family transferred the patient to another hospital, and the father never responded to the family consultant's efforts to communicate with him.

Sometimes intolerance of ambiguity is revealed by the rigidity, tending to the bizarre, with which family myths are maintained. In the earlier example of Bernard, the symphony conductor's son, intensive analytic work with the patient for a decade, plus direct contact with members of his family when the patient was hospitalized, revealed to the therapist the rigidity of several family myths and the extent to which the father was seen as a frozen mythical figure. At first the paradox arising from this situation seemed impressive, for on the one hand the family assigned the only and ultimate value to the grandeur and untouchability of the paternal figure, and on the other hand they reinforced the taboo against emulating it. This paradox is not so unusual, however, if we consider it against the background of the patriarchal culture from which the family came. Attempts by the therapist to discuss with the patient's mother the no-win situation in which her son was placed met with blank stares and total incomprehension. Such a possibility was simply not in the accepted script. When the therapist then tried to approach the matter indirectly, by discussing the lives of various family members, he repeatedly encountered the style of defending the untouchability of the myth, as illustrated by the following example.

The patient's mother was describing how her now-deceased husband had been determined to pursue his own inspired musical career despite the tremendous pressure placed on him by his own family to follow a technical career. With great emphasis, she said that on the same day on which he was supposed to register for a technical course in his hometown he went instead to register at the musical conservatory in the city of X. The therapist, indicating that the clarification of minor matters can sometimes be of importance in connection with therapy, asked if it was possible that he registered a few days later, since the city of X is a great distance from the hometown. "No," she said, again emphatically, "he took a plane so he could do it the same day." Although this supposed event occurred long before the era of commercial aviation, the "same day" of registration was part of the literal and verbatim untouchable family myth and could therefore not be tampered with even if the recital of surrounding circumstances had to be distorted. For that family, mythical structures could not be approached with the playful ambiguity to which they are particularly vulnerable. Herein lies the connecting link between the life-and-death seriousness of the defense of the family myth and the problem of tolerance of ambiguity. The child prepared to deal only with rigid myths is poorly prepared to deal with living beings and live experiences.

In a sense, the timeless rigidity of such a defensively perpetuated mythical being or object is the opposite of the fluidity of play, of the toy, of the transitional object (Smith, 1983; Winnicott, 1958). A lack of preparation for the necessary integration of ambiguous experience was also the common element in the following two cases, which will be reported in more detail in a later chapter. The *uncanniness* that characterized the experiences of a self-mutilator, Mary, and of Anna, a patient who had many déjà vu sensations, could be traced to paradoxical experiences for which they were especially ill prepared.

The term *uncanny* (Freud, 1919) is an appropriate descriptive word for the feelings that Mary conveyed about her state just prior to cutting. Her sense of uncanniness was related to contrasting convictions, both equally strong, that she must somehow be alive but that at the same time she did not feel alive. Cutting was an escape from this intolerable burden of ambiguity.

I have now come to see that she used her own body as a transitional object—transitional in this case between animate and inanimate—and that this was a special case of an attempt to work on what Winnicott calls the "perpetual human task of keeping inner and outer reality separate yet interrelated." Winnicott's development of the theme that a "neutral area of experience which will not be challenged" is important during specific development phases—he says the pattern of transitional phenomena begins to show at somewhere between four and twelve months (p. 232)—is congruent with the theme being developed here. Experience that will "not be challenged," which seems to me to correspond to the tolerance of ambiguity, permits the gradual formation of an attitudinal "membrane" which is egosyntonic to the extent that it has not been prematurely and externally imposed but has been individually established through much active exploratory crossing and recrossing of cultural border territory that is poorly or ambiguously defined. In my work with Mary, I experienced some sadistic feelings that I believe were at times an escape for me from *my* uncanny experiences, which were triggered by my contact with her. These uncanny experiences were related, I believe, to the patient's "undigested," dissociated transitional states involving the animate versus "inanimate" nature of her own body, to which I shall return later.

Anna, the patient who reported many déjà vu experiences and who came to psychoanalysis in connection with hysterical fugue states, experienced minor repetitions of such states during her sessions. The consistent association of synesthetic and déjà vu phenomena in her case (which will be described later in some detail) led me to develop (Kafka, 1966) the following formulation in an attempt to explain this connection. As a schematic introduction to the idea, imagine that a particular wave pattern on an oscilloscope represents visual, auditory, or tactile stimuli. A responding organism or electronic scanning machine is then asked if this is a familiar *visual* pattern. Obviously, if the response is to the *pattern*, whatever the sensory modality involved, the likelihood that it will be familiar is much increased. That is, a déjà vu or related sensation will be aroused if the pattern of the visual stimulation evokes a corresponding echo in *any* other sensory compartment, be it auditory, tactile, or the like. In other words, if a certain pattern of stimulation, let us say a visual pattern, occurs at a time when the sensory compartments are particularly interwoven, particularly blended, the chances that the pattern will arouse a feeling of familiarity are multiplied.

Schachtel (1947) has eloquently developed the theme that infantile amnesia is related *not* to the content of early infantile experiences but to the fact that the schemata of experience are different from the adult ones. Synesthesia is more characteristic of early experiences, and sensory compartmentalization is more characteristic of later ones. In chapter 3 I will report detailed clinical evidence that the patient who had many déjà vu sensations had experienced premature demands for task-oriented behavior involving sensory compartmentalization at times when playful, "dreamy" synesthetic experience was wished for and would have been more appropriate. I came to conceptualize some of her difficulties as related to insufficient opportunity to cross and recross without challenge the transitional area between synesthesia and sensory compartmentalization.

The experience of uncanniness, of weirdness, of something unearthly or supernatural, is produced when our experience cannot be dismissed—when it carries conviction, but does not make sense. Two contradictory experiences, both convincing and thus affectively charged, result in the sensation of uncanniness. The uncanny affect of the déjà vu experience ("I just caught myself experiencing something as familiar which I know is not familiar") has a similarity to the slightly uncanny affect one experiences after having been trapped by reading the sign "Ignore this sign." If feelings of uncanniness are understood as occurring when typically ambiguous experiences of about equally convincing strength are present simultaneously, we can see that this condition is met in the déjà vu experience. One doubts one's senses, one has trouble with one's "me-ness." I no longer believe that synesthesia is necessarily involved in déjà vu experiences, but I still believe that some ambiguity—be it sensory blending versus sensory compartmentalization, animate versus inanimate, linear versus nonlinear systems of "causality," or some other source—may be particularly strange and unacceptable to individuals of whom well-compartmentalized behavior was demanded at a time when parents usually fulfill this function and permit the child to indulge without danger in the richness of blending and other ambiguous experiences.

As I shall elaborate later, for the self-mutilator and for the patient with fugue states and déjà vu experiences, therapy involved processes of reacceptance of, or perhaps acceptance of, or more specifically a *learning to be less unfamiliar with*, feelings of estrangement from their usual way of experiencing the world. The fear component of the experience of awe which accompanies the simultaneous sense of familiarity and unfamiliarity is diminished. The uncanny comes to contain less dread. In my work with hospitalized patients (Kafka and McDonald, 1965; Kafka, 1966), the risk that the patient will be removed from treatment by a parent highly intolerant of ambiguity has led me to work with families in ways that combine necessary myth breaking with precautionary measures. These techniques include contact with a large number of family members and the selective joint interviewing of individuals who have avoided being alone with each other (see chapter 6). If, for instance, it is observed that whenever a joint interview of daughter and father is scheduled, one or the other becomes sick, has a pressing business appointment, or finds some other means to cancel the scheduled session, a special effort is made to understand and overcome this avoidance. Such specific resistance often is the door behind which a family myth is hidden.

Comment

Formal and clinical considerations of two kinds of conflicting communication—contradictions, which *theoretically* involve one level of abstraction, and paradoxes or ambiguities, which involve more than one level—have led me to the belief that human experience and interaction always involve more than one level of abstraction. *Subjectively*, people tend to react to conflicting material that involves distances in levels of abstraction for which they are prepared by seeing it as contradictory and associating it with feelings of ambivalence, particularly when the contradictory pulls are of approximately equal strength. Conflicting material involving distances in levels of abstraction for which people are *not* prepared are seen as paradoxical or ambiguous and are associated with experiences of dissonance, of uncanniness, various degrees of loss of feelings of "me-ness," or depersonalization—particularly when the conflicting data are of approximately equal strength (as in déjà vu).

All human living involves considerable paradoxical experience and struggle with paradoxical systems that represent reality (from mild déjà vu sensations to wave versus particle theory). More centrally, individuation without alienation involves the development of personal "realities" that incorporate paradoxical discontinuities from maternal or parental realities. In the reformulation that I am emphasizing here, parental tolerance of ambiguity—communicated in a style, to a degree, and with timing appropriate for the developmental level of the child—is conceptualized as necessary for the offspring's individuation and for the prevention of "pathologic" degrees of "splitting," alienation, and dissonance. Such a beneficial, nonpathogenic tolerance must be embedded in a communication system in which an anchoring in a reality common to parent, child, and culture has been achieved—an overlap in the child's, the family's, and the larger society's "subjective equivalences" or in their levels of abstraction.

Such formulations relating to the positive aspects of ambiguity have implications for research and therapeutic conceptualizations. As I described earlier, our attempts to identify parents or parents-to-be who were pathogenic double-binders were not successful—probably in part because of the difficulties inherent in double-bind theory. In a related area of investigation, Ryder and Goodrich (Ryder, 1966, 1968, 1969; Ryder and Goodrich, 1966; Goodrich and Boomer, 1963) generated interaction test data concerning the modes of behavior of couples confronted with irreconcilable information. Spouses were given a "color-matching test," with instructions implying that the experimenter was interested in visual functions. Sitting opposite each other, the spouses faced panels containing individually numbered fields of color. The husband's panel was not visible to the wife and hers was not visible to him. Presumably the panels were identical, and, indeed, when both were asked, for instance, to name the color associated with the number 4, both said "dark purple." From time to time, however, the experimental subjects encountered a situation in which the number and the color on the two panels did not match. Subjects in these experiments may decide, for instance, that their spouses or the experimenters are tricking them, they may doubt their own functioning, they may to varying degrees leave the question open, and they may or may not communicate about their doubts or tentative conclusions. In terms of the formulations advanced here, I would hypothesize that couples and/or individuals whose task performance deteriorates when they are confronted with irreconcilable data *and* who do not metacommunicate about the paradoxical situation in which they find themselves might be expected to deal poorly with their individuating offspring if the children confront them with reality experiences paradoxical to their own. The merits of any such prediction concerning parental help or interference with individuation, of course, hinge on the extent to which performance in a laboratory task with one's spouse is predictive of naturalistic behavior with one's child. Attempts to rate ambiguity tolerance in interview material are still crude but may be of some limited use. Some adaptations of Berlyne's (1966) experimental techniques to determine the optimum ambiguity range—optimum for the maintenance of interest—might also be useful in identifying parents with wide and narrow optimum ranges (Hohage and Kuebler, 1985).

In the framework of the reformulation being proposed here, the therapeutic double bind is conceptualized more parsimoniously than in the original theory, as a kind of replacement in therapy of what was missing during crucial developmental phases—that is, adequate exposure to paradoxes that prepare the person for life as a separate and unique individual, paradoxes that I see as an essential component of the very process of individuation. This therapeutic application of ambiguity does not imply any planned or calculated use of paradox or irrationality. Rather, it refers to handling of the ambiguities that naturally emerge in the flow and counterflow of transference and countertransference in the relationship by the use of communications and metacommunications that are appropriate to the mixture of developmental levels characterizing both the patient and the therapist.

The temporal dimension of multiple-reality organizations is not specifically addressed by double-bind theorists and did not play a part in my critique and reformulation of the hypothesis. Gradually, however, obvious temporal reference in the very notion of object *constancy* led me to a synthetic view of the themes of multiple realities and time, which are discussed in the next chapter.

Chapter 3

Déjà Vu, Drugs, Synesthesia,
and the Mind-Time Synthesis

In a psychiatric context, the ancient philosophical problem of the nature of reality tends to lose much of its abstract quality and to gain a personal poignancy, because estrangement—alienation from reality—may mean tragic personal isolation. The central importance of time will emerge as we continue to examine, from clinical, experimental, and theoretical perspectives, the phenomena related to estrangement from consensually validated reality.

In the previous chapter, I discussed Klüver's (1936) use of the concept of subjectively equivalent stimuli in studying the building blocks of psychological reality. I will continue to relate some of his formulations to clinical data and to psychoanalytic concepts by elaborating their relevance not only to an understanding of object constancy (Kafka, 1964) but to the related issues of ambiguity, paradox, and time.

Although Freud dealt with issues of misperception of reality, especially misperception of the difference between male and female genitalia, for him there was basically one (commonsense) reality, which is or is not perceived correctly. Hartmann (1939) deals with some aspects of the relativity of reality, but for him this relativity is circumscribed—he still finds a fairly solid foothold in an "average expectable environment." Such stability, even though

limited, becomes acutely problematic for such authors as Loewald, Wallerstein, Novey, and Lichtenstein. They differ in their
emphases on developmental, social, or psychic structural issues
and in the degree to which they see the social and intrapsychic
structural-reality problems as separate or related. But they share
such concerns as the collapse of ideas about commonsense reality,
the crisis in consensual validation, and the waning of agreement on
the average expectable environment. Novey (1955) goes so far as
to emphasize the fundamental similarity between "normal" ordered reality systems and delusional systems.

Lichtenstein traces "the transformation of 'reality' since
Freud" (1974, p. 353) and illustrates with case material the
"changing function of the id" (p. 358) and of the superego that
results from a radical alteration of reality perception. With reference to the id, Lichtenstein says, "To use the sexual experience in
the service of a desperate effort at affirmation of the reality of the
self and the other . . . is a shift in the function of psychic structures" (p. 360). With reference to the superego, he describes a
patient who was not schizophrenic but who, after some experi-
menting with psychedelic drugs, began to feel that there were
really no objects, that everything was force—energy that flowed
through what was living and what was not living, in unbroken
waves or vibrations. She began to read articles on modern physics
in *Scientific American*, which bore out her feeling that there was no
such thing as objectivity or mechanistic laws, and that the ordinary
reality of everyday life represented only one limited dimension of
what was real. She was, however, unable to bridge the inner gap
between a reality perception that, as she said, absorbed her into an
inner space and the competitive world around her. She felt temporarily at peace when she could be in touch with nature, but she
yearned for a shared life with others, emotional contact, and
meaningful communication, and this, more and more, evaded her
(p. 363).

Keeping Lichtenstein's description in mind, let us return to the
notion of object constancy and its connection to subjective equivalence. As I commented in chapter 2, in psychoanalysis, object
constancy usually refers to the coalescence of partially conflicting
images—for example, the bringing together of the images of the

gratifying "good" mother and the frustrating "bad" mother into one internal representation of a mother figure. Anna Freud, in an address at the International Psychoanalytic Congress in Vienna in 1971, spoke of the ability to maintain object constancy as the ability to continue to love the frustrating object.

Before proceeding, I wish to point out that Klüver's "subjective equivalence" can be used not only in reference to object constancy—that is, to the identity of objects—but also in reference to time. Many of the clinical and experimental data on time discussed in chapter 1 are elaborations of the everyday observation that time passes faster on some occasions and more slowly on others. This must mean that *objectively different* time spans can be *subjectively equivalent*.

For Lichtenstein's patient, there were "really no objects" since no one pattern of subjective equivalence was consistently dominant. She was *aware* of a kind of floating energy or force flowing in waves through both inanimate and animate objects and creating, in rapid succession, different patterns of subjective equivalence. This description is congruent with clinical distinctions (Kafka, 1964) between subject and object, between self and nonself, which may disappear or recede into the background because of the subjective equivalence of some fragmentary self-representations with fragmentary mental representations of others. I have encountered analogous issues in investigations of psychotic phenomena and psychedelic drug experiences (Kafka, 1964; Kafka and Gaarder, 1964). In Lichtenstein's patient such blurring of borders apparently made communication difficult with those around her, who perceived the world differently—that is, in terms of more stable, more lastingly differentiated objects.

Other influences on the formation of a system of subjective equivalences are motivational factors—the drive organization and its current state of activation. The organization of patterns of subjective equivalence is obviously related in some way to the nature of early object relations. In addition, for the development of stable patterns of object constancy in the psychoanalytic sense, relatively stable patterns of object constancy in the "perceptual" sense are almost certainly necessary. The two meanings of the term have overlapping elements arising out of the same matrix. The study of drugs that profoundly affect perceptual processes has yielded some particularly pertinent data. My own participation in studies of two substances with very different effects, LSD and Serynl, has provided me with useful illustrative material.

Illustrations from the Study of LSD

If perceptual processes are closely linked to object constancy, the distinction between compartmentalization and synesthetic perception becomes of great interest. Synesthesia, as I have noted, means the blending of sensory modalities—for example, the mental linking of colors with music or other sounds.

Before LSD became a street drug, I took part in an organized research program on psychedelic substances with several psychoanalyst colleagues who worked with psychotic patients. We took LSD on Sunday, saw patients on Monday, and studied some effects of the LSD experience on the therapeutic work. I want to emphasize that research with the substances we used was authorized at that time and that we did not see patients while acutely under the influence of the drug. We specifically wanted to investigate if the memory of an experience with a drug thought to mimic psychotic experience would facilitate our understanding of and therapeutic work with psychotic patients.

Some of my fellow therapists felt that the LSD experience had no effect on their therapeutic work, and we all recognized that a multiplicity of factors, including the social setting, can influence an LSD experience, which can range from ecstatic delight to profound terror. Nevertheless, we felt that some generalizations could be attempted since some similar formal characteristics of the experience had been described by many LSD subjects. They felt in tune with each other, although the experiences were intensely personal and were reported as such. The awareness of a common chord—an awareness that was a necessary consequence of the multidimensionality of the LSD experience—seemed to be the formal characteristic about which generalization was most justified.

An extensive literature already existed on LSD-25 and related drugs, but there were not many recent psychodynamic studies of those substances. A comprehensive review of the literature published by Unger (1963) revealed that differences between the drug-induced state and naturally occurring psychopathologic conditions had been stressed (Hoch et al., 1958). But LSD-induced ego states (Savage, 1955) *congruent* with some aspects of naturally occurring psychopathology had also been described and called to the attention of psychotherapists. Investigators of LSD action expressed the opinion (Abramson, 1959) that anyone who attempted to use LSD as a therapeutic tool should himself have experienced the effects of the drug. In our search of the literature, however, we had not found studies dealing specifically with the effects of the psychotherapist's LSD or other psychotomimetic experience on his subsequent therapeutic work.

Direct observations were made on five psychotherapists who took doses of 75 to 250 micrograms of LSD-25 after appropriate medical screening. Two of the psychotherapists took LSD-25 on two occasions, and three took it once. Although larger dosages were generally associated with more intense effects, in our limited experience neither repetition nor dosage variation systematically altered the pattern of the drug experience or the pattern of its effect on subsequent therapeutic work. Complete medical facilities, an observing physician and nurse, and tape recordings of the drug sessions were provided. Some psychotherapy sessions following the therapist's LSD experiences were tape-recorded, as were a series of clinical discussions among the five experimental subjects. In addition, they discussed their experiences with eight other psychotherapists who had had LSD experiences elsewhere. In preparing the study for publication, we attempted to present a distillate of trends in our own observations and in those of others (Kafka and Gaarder, 1964).

We described two classes of effects on the therapist's work. The first concerned the more immediate, more spontaneous, less thought-through effects—perhaps those which the therapist himself might notice with some surprise. The second class comprised theorizing stimulated by the more spontaneous LSD effects.

Although the richness of the experience makes one uncomfortable with any summarizing statements, we did attempt some generalizations about the phenomenology of LSD. Much of it can be described in terms of a collapse of the categories of formal logic. Under LSD the subject experiences himself as A and B at the same time—for example, as a self-observer in a drug experiment and simultaneously as a line in a musical structure. The multiple layers of experience, the multiple levels of meaning, all seem to him to be equally valid, even though the subject is aware that only one of the levels of meaning is accepted as the appropriate one by his colleagues who are not under the influence of the drug.

To what extent can LSD produce schizophrenialike states? One therapist under LSD said, "I know this is such-and-such a place and such-and-such a date, but all this doesn't have the significance you ascribe to it." Somewhat similar comments are occasionally made by schizophrenic patients when they show clinical improvement. Peter, about whom I will say more in chapter 5, could differentiate the hallucinated voices of father and God, but found the distinction of no significance to him. Furthermore some regressed schizophrenic patients behave appropriately in such situations as a fire in the hospital unit. This may illustrate both their access to information and the selectivity of their responses to stimuli and situations that also "make a difference" in their framework. In a high percentage of cases (but not in all of them), observers can correctly distinguish tape-recorded LSD interviews from similar interviews with schizophrenic patients (Abramson, 1959). Investigating the characteristics of the exceptions—the patients who cannot be distinguished from the LSD subjects— might yield enlightening results.

To return now to the main theme here—the effects of the LSD experience on the therapists' work with patients—first, the multidimensionality of their LSD experiences diminished the "either-or" type of questions that several therapists asked of their patients. In trying to describe the multidimensionality of the LSD world, we found it useful to use an extended concept of synesthesia, which goes beyond the usual sensory synesthesia of seeing, hearing, tactile sense, kinesthesia, and temperature sense to include mood, emotion, space, and time. In a world in which the distinction between subject and object has disappeared, the feeling of one's body is in constant flux—for example, one may feel a surface becoming an S-shaped line as in a surrealist movie, and a line coming toward one splitting up into time. One may feel primary energy before it has taken on the form of any specific sensory modality.

After experiencing this "multidimensionality in all directions," this collapse of logical categories, one therapist felt that he could understand why patients, particularly psychotic patients, had previously reacted to either-or questions as though they were somewhat insulting and inappropriate. For example, while working with a delusional, hallucinated psychotic patient whose gestures and words had often indicated that people were putting thoughts into her head or taking them out, he had often found himself curious about specific aspects of this experience: did her skull seem to soften? did the hand reach in? and so on. It did not occur to the therapist to pursue this kind of questioning with every delusional and hallucinated patient, but it had in this case because of her specific intonations and gestures. After he had taken LSD, however, his curiosity about how the patient experienced the putting in and taking out of thoughts seemed an idiotic preoccupation. Acknowledging that to the patient led to a widening of the field of therapeutic communication.

The therapist's experience of simultaneous multiplicity of meaning and particularly of synesthesia in the extended sense also led to another LSD-connected development in therapy with the same patient. An endless and exasperating repetitiveness characterized some of her psychotherapy hours. At one point she explained that she repeated what she said (which was usually requests) and did not respond to answers, questions, or discussions in order not to lose the trend of her thought and also not to lose her self, not to lose her identity, not to lose her goals. Weeks after this explanation, the patient exhibited a curious pattern of behavior. When she complained that she was being mauled and manhandled by the ward personnel, the staff pointed out that she had initiated a pattern of planting herself in front of doors or in passageways, always "in the way" of someone. The therapist's LSD experience of "verbal-postural synesthesia" helped him equate this behavior with her repetitive verbal behavior. He told her that apparently one meaning of her behavior was a physical statement of "I am here— this is me, this is me," and so forth. The patient seemed pleased and complimented him by saying, "This is a very beautiful ash-tray—did you make it?"

For some of the therapists in our experiment, several facets of the LSD experience contributed to a greater tolerance for silence in the hours. One was the feeling of the inappropriateness of many either-or questions. Possibly, also, a blurring of the distinction between animate and inanimate objects during phases of the LSD experience was a factor. For one therapist, some voices, for instance, seemed to be mechanical and dead, whereas certain objects—like the bedstead that hc was gripping while affected by LSD—were experienced as full of living energy. The "physiognomy" of furniture, a pattern in the rug, and the like provided such an overwhelmingly rich experience that after having taken LSD, and particularly in the presence of a patient who seemed to respond to the physiognomy of objects, he was more willing to join the patient in silent experience of the environment. One patient repeatedly asked him to come to her room so that she could "explain things" to him but would invariably fall silent when he complied. His LSD experience of the richness of the physiognomy of objects made this behavior seem less bizarre, since he could assume that she was silently asking him to share such richness.

An increase of confidence in the accuracy of social perceptions during the LSD experience, and for at least some time thereafter, could also contribute to the acceptance of silence. In at least one instance such confidence even contributed to the therapist's issuing a sharply worded request to the patient to be silent. The day after he had taken LSD, while working with a neurotic patient, he felt much more certain than on other occasions that the patient, although mouthing many words, was not "communicating meaningfully." Somewhat to his own surprise, he heard himself telling the patient emphatically to be quiet when he really had nothing to say. The startled patient responded with a four-letter word, became silent for almost twenty minutes, and then started to communicate more thoughtfully and meaningfully.

Because of an LSD experience of panic about the disintegrative threat, one therapist became freer in having vigorous physical contact with some psychotic patients when they were struggling against impending loss of contact. He became very skeptical about notions that the psychotic patient is easily threatened by the therapist, since in his recent LSD experience he had recognized that the terror of losing contact is immeasurably greater than the fear of hostile contact. In addition to using more physical contact with psychotic patients, he made more liberal use of wet-sheet packs as an "orienting" restraint during therapy hours.

Some of the therapists noted that when they were under the influence of the drug, the pattern of their whole experiential world could ᴜe shattered by a sudden noise, such as a sneeze. This led them to become more alert to a patient's behavioral changes following the occurrence of a sudden stimulus. That a sudden kaleidoscopic shift from one world into another is a recurrent event for some psychotic patients is a hypothesis for which there is much clinical evidence. It is our impression that the kaleidoscopic changes of the LSD experience and of some schizophrenic conditions are phenomenologically similar. After our LSD experience, we felt that some schizophrenic patients sensed that their therapists had to some extent "been there" and could recognize an altered, easily shattered world, and that this widened the area of communication.

Like our specific changes in clinical technique following the LSD experience, our related *theorizing* about therapeutic concepts was rooted in the multidimensionality of the LSD experience. Although it was described in many different ways, the richness of meaning of all events, perceptions, and experiences was generally commented upon by subjects taking LSD.

Because at times the LSD richness may have a driving quality—"I can't keep up with it"—one of the theories we formulated hypothesizes that hebephrenic silliness is an understandable escape from meaning. The conviction that meaning itself, in its formal characteristics, can be threatening may well influence therapeutic work with hebephrenic patients. Before taking LSD one therapist felt that he might have been much too concerned with content in treating a hebephrenic patient, overcautiously staying with the patient in the area judged to be less anxiety-producing than most others, the area where the patient could communicate with "silliness." After the specific recognition that *formal* qualities of meaning can be threatening, the therapist was more likely to

experience the patient's acceptance of meaning as a monumental
vote of confidence in the relationship as it existed at that moment.
Had not the patient, out of despair or trust or both, accepted the
therapist's kind of meaning as his own, when previously an over-
whelming number of kinds of meaning had been equally valid for
him? With greater ease and with less caution concerning the
content of the communication, the therapist could then exploit the
temporary acceptance of meaning—of secondary process, one
might say—by the patient.

Another theoretical notion that can affect therapeutic work is
related to the fluctuations experienced by the LSD subject, in and
out of various levels of loss of ego control and reality contact. The
LSD experience reinforced our familiar preoccupation with the
question of whether or not a patient, especially a psychotic patient,
is in voluntary control of a particular symptom. One of the therapists who took LSD felt at times that there was only one point in
which he was one up on the colleague and the nurse who were with
him during the experiment—namely, that he knew better than they
did when he was more or less "gone." He was very reluctant to
give up this secret. Some time after his LSD experience, when he
was in doubt about the voluntary components of psychotic symptoms in a patient, he expressed his doubts to the patient but now
also put into words his recognition of the patient's need to be ahead
of him, to be one up in this respect. His expressed acceptance of
the patient's need for this secret apparently produced a twinkle of
recognition in the patient and maintained some continuity of communication at a time in therapy when communication was extremely tenuous.

Although our work with psychotics provided us with the most
explicit examples of effects of the LSD experience on our therapy
techniques, we also felt that the experience had considerable, less
explicit effect on our work with nonpsychotic patients. For example, observations of our own post-LSD dreams led us to pay more
attention to what we called the dimension of "abstract expressionism" in dreams reported by neurotic patients, by which we mean
the degree of feeling and rich emotional meaning carried by an
abstract and formal pattern (Kafka and Gaarder, 1964).

After the LSD experience one therapist had dreams unusual for him in their formal characteristics. He dreamed, for instance, about "an almost but not completely smooth, progressing line, with one of the small wiggles in it representing the Nazi period and six million Jews killed." Upon awakening he felt that he had dreamed and experienced the "expanse of history." Gradually, after the LSD experience, the formal characteristics of his dreams returned to their more usual pattern.

We speculate that perhaps a greater emotional meaning invested in abstract pattern in dreams of our patients corresponded to what would be described in Rorschach terminology as a more dilated *Erlebnistyp*—that is, an increase in kinesthetic and color-determined responses. We further conjectured that more feeling associated with abstract patterns in dreams of neurotic patients might correspond to a loosening of defensive structures. After our LSD experience, we paid more attention to these possible meanings of the dimension of abstract expressionism in patients' dreams.

In generalizing about the effects of our LSD experience on our therapeutic work, we were aware that much of what we had described was in tune with the zeitgeist of phenomenologic and existential awareness in psychiatry and was not necessarily and exclusively related to psychotomimetic drugs. Nevertheless, we believed that our attempt to study such effects had enriched our knowledge of therapy, therapists, and psychopathology as well as the phenomenology of drugs. Some of the effects may have been simply the result of a new and dramatic experience, whether traumatic or pleasurable, or of the therapist's greater insight into previously less exposed areas of his functioning; some may have been related to the confrontation with techniques for holding onto reality and consequent diminution of anxiety; and some may have resulted from the sharing with our patients of a world in which the selective filtering that we call secondary-process functioning operated less than in most other situations. In our study we did not consider some broader questions concerning therapeutic uses of psychotomimetic substances—for example, the usefulness to patients in psychotherapy of taking these substances; the possibility of therapist and patient simultaneously taking the drugs; or the effects of a drugged therapist, with or without a cotherapist, seeing the patient. Investigation of these broader issues would involve the question of whether these techniques permit exploration beyond the secondary process while at the same time permitting self-observation, communication, and integration.

To summarize our LSD study, undertaken at a time when LSD was more widely legally approved as a research tool and was not yet a street drug, we distinguished the following immediate effects of the therapist's LSD experience and a few later, more theoretical ones. The collapse of logical categories, the multidimensionality of the experience, blurring of the borders between animate and inanimate objects, the importance of the physiognomy of objects, and increased confidence in social perception were believed to be among the factors leading to diminution of either-or questions. Increased attention to the physiognomy of objects and greater sensitivity to communication through posture or actual position in space led to an extension of nonverbal communication and therefore to greater tolerance for silence. More theoretical notions included the idea that hebephrenic silliness may be an attempt to escape the threat of the richness and multiplicity of meaning and the idea that some patients may need to obscure the degree to which they fluctuate in and out of psychosis in order to be secretly one up on nonpsychotic persons, who have the advantage of a stable reference structure.

Illustrations from the Study of Sernyl

In another part of our study of the effects of therapists' drug experience on their understanding of and therapeutic work with patients, Dr. Kenneth Gaarder took the drug Sernyl (1-[1-phenylcyclohexyl] piperidine HCL) by intravenous injection; I served as the principal observer of his reactions. Sernyl's chemical structure, neurophysiological mechanisms, and psychological effects are completely different from those of the LSD-mescaline-psilocybin group of drugs.[1] When Gaarder reported on the work in a Chestnut Lodge symposium in the fall of 1963

1. For recent studies of PCP and mental processes, see Mark S. Sonders, John F. W. Keana, and Eckard Weber, "Phencyclidine and Psychotomimetic Sigma Opiates: Recent Insights into Their Biochemical and Physiological Sites of Action," *Trends in Neuro-Science* 10 (1987): 263–302; 11 (1988): 37–40.

(Gaarder and Kafka, 1963), we had no idea that the study would be among the last authorized human experiments with this dangerous substance, now better known as PCP. In our unpublished report, from which I will quote extensively, we were attempting to serve two functions. First, we wanted to contribute to general knowledge about an important new mode of producing psychotomimetic effects. Second, we wished to report a finding about the phenomenology of the Sernyl experience that had not been previously observed.

In describing Gaarder's reactions, we made certain assumptions: that both schizophrenics and psychotomimetic drug subjects undergo a *multiplicity* of experiences in which there are profound alterations of the ego; that these can be described as a series of "ego states," which are often strikingly different from one another; that within each state there is a particular organization of the cathectic forces of the ego, differing from that of other states in the quality and quantity invested in the various agencies of the ego; that there are transitional stages in which the ego and its energies are involved in change from one state to another; and that the study of psychotomimetic states, transitions between states, and the intervention by which these states and transitions may be altered can be a means to further understanding of ego states and transitions between them in general.

In the meager psychiatric literature concerning Sernyl, it is usually described as having the unique property of selectively inhibiting the function of the sensory system. Thus, its main effect is to produce the equivalent of sensory deprivation rapidly, without the need for isolation apparatuses. All sense modalities are inhibited without primary toxic effects on consciousness, thinking, or motor activity. With increasing dosage of Sernyl, there is a gradual loss of peripheral sensations—pain, the sense of position, and so on—and of such senses as vision and hearing. Largely on the basis of clinical neurological examination of subjects, investigators have deduced that the site of action of Sernyl is the primary sensory center of the body, the thalamus, although the midbrain and sensory cortex are also implicated (Meyer et al., 1959; Luby et al., 1959). Authors differ in their interpretation of the relative importance of Sernyl's effects on internal versus external sensations. Those who have studied the drug as an anesthetic agent for surgery have no question about its capacity to diminish external perception (Meyer et al., 1959). Those who have studied it in combination with sensory deprivation by apparatus stress the loss of internal perception (Luby et al., 1959; Pollard et al., 1960) because a person who has taken Sernyl experiences fewer symptoms and less distress when isolated than when in an unrestricted environment.

As with sensory deprivation, important effects on thought processes and motor behavior occur secondarily until with high doses the subject is in a catatonic trance. Other major effects observed at various doses are the feeling that one's body parts do not belong to oneself; a subjective feeling of being dead; the inability to conceptualize and carry on complex conversations; and loss of the sense of the presence of the unvisualized visual environment and also of tunnel vision, so that existing visual space is a small circle in front of the subject. Sernyl proved unsatisfactory as a surgical anesthetic because these effects complicated the postoperative course with transient psychotic episodes. Sernyl has also been observed to produce acute discomfort and agitation in chronic schizophrenic patients. It has been tolerated better by children and older people than by young adults (Meyer et al., 1959; Luby et al., 1959; Pollard et al., 1960).

In summary, Sernyl makes it possible to study the interrelationships of enteroception, exteroception, body image, thought processes, motor activity, and reality constructs as they combine dynamically to create the living ego. Studying Sernyl became particularly important in exploring schizophrenia in the light of Gaarder's hypothesis that schizophrenic thought disorder is the result of sensory deprivation to which the patient has contributed by interpersonal and intrapsychic mechanisms (Gaarder, 1963).

Our observations were confined to a single subject (Gaarder) who took a relatively small dose (3.3 mgm intravenous [0.05 mgm/kg body weight]) just once. Gaarder was well acquainted with the literature about Sernyl but had not seen the drug in use. The effects began within ten minutes after the injection of the drug and were over within forty-five minutes. They were followed by several hours of a hangover type of hypersensitivity to noise.

In the following excerpts from the tape recording of my exchanges with Gaarder at the height of the experience, note the dullness, the thinking difficulty, the bewilderment about existential questions, and the lack of interpersonal sensitivity revealed in his responses.

KG: . . . something is going on here and uh—uh—I'm alive—and uh—I'm doing something for some reason, and I don't know what it is I'm doing and uh—what's happening to me now—and words are things like that what is happening?—what is to say what is happening? is a word—and people talk—and what is talking?—and uh—I don't know what's going on. . . .

KG: . . . I'm a person in a—there's a time-place continuum—and uh—something is going on here—what it's all about I don't know and who I am and where and how and all that kind of thing and I'm in an office—and an office is a thing which people sit in because they want to talk to one another and Sigmund—Sigmund Freud—I haven't thought about Sigmund Freud for a while—Sigmund Freud is a man who figured out something—oh—uh—I don't know. What's a psychiatrist? It's very [laughs]—it's a very interesting experience. I'm experiencing something and I don't know what's going on, and I don't know what saying what's going on is saying. . . .

KG: . . . uh—am I alive? Or—what's alive?

JK: You're alive—whatever it is.

KG: What is it?

JK: Hell—you take this drug so you can tell us! You took a drug.

KG: Who? Me? [Laughs]

JK: You.

KG: When?

JK: How long ago do you think you took it?

KG: Let's see—let's see—I took a drug in—oh—about fifteen minutes ago, I guess—didn't I?

JK: How did you figure out the time?

KG: Have I been talking quite a bit?

JK: Mmm-hmm.

KG: Good! Well—whatever else happens at least I'll know what I said—but who am I?—what am I doing? I mean why am I—uh—what's going on?

RM [TECHNICIAN]: I'm going to take your blood pressure, Ken.

JK: Would it make you feel better if I tell you what's going on? Do you want to know?

KG: Yeah.

JK: You took Sernyl—that's a drug you're interested in—you're a psychiatrist, and you took this Sernyl to see how it makes you feel, and you're under the influence of that drug right now.

In the literature on Sernyl, the subject is usually described as being strongly aware of a strikingly altered body image, characterized by feelings of floating away from one's own body or of being dead and being a corpse, with a profound subjective awareness of this as *bodily experience* (Bakker and Amini, 1961). It is of interest that Gaarder did not have such an experience. Although he was aware of the possibility of its occurrence from his previous reading, he was to a high degree set in an intellectual, conceptualizing mode as he underwent the experience. Aware of the apathy of subjects described in the literature, he was determined to keep talking about what was happening so that the tape recording of his experience would have sufficient material on it. In addition, the self-imposed structure and activity of language may have had an important effect in limiting the extent of his disorientation. Whatever the reason, he did not experience loss of body image but instead wondered intellectually if he were alive or not; he was unaware of his body in the way a person is when intensely involved in other spheres.

Gaarder's salient experience, both at the time he took the drug (as tape-recorded) and retrospectively, was a profound change in thinking in which there was a loss of the meaning of logical categories and of the experience of causal relationships. He retained all the essential "facts" about himself and his situation at the moment—time, place, person, role, and a memory of having seen several patients and a supervisor that morning—but he was unable to establish relationships between these facts and was bewildered about them. Just as others who are described in the Sernyl literature profoundly believed that their body-image experiences were real, to the same degree Gaarder reported feeling profound bewilderment about the questions he posed. Perhaps he kept repeating the questions as a means of maintaining contact.

Because Gaarder had also taken LSD, he was able to contrast the experiences. He felt that in both there was a loss of the relatively restricted and narrowly channeled logical connections that characterize the more usual, "normal" modes of thinking. However, whereas LSD enabled him to see the richness and multiplicity of diverse meanings of relationships between things and was a "creative" experience, taking Sernyl resulted in a loss of meanings of relationships between things and was a bewildering experience.

The general lack of richness of the Sernyl experience was manifested in three other areas. The first was the subject's feeling that *he did not care much about the interaction with his observers* and was not terribly affected by the subtleties of what they did and said; in order for them to have a very striking effect on him they had to put their message across very forcefully. The psychological heaviness, the lack of subtle modulation of thought and feeling, was strikingly contagious to the observer, who felt that dull repetition of orienting statements was useful to the subject, perhaps especially so if accompanied by some physical contact. This was in striking contrast to the LSD experience, in which the observer was easily caught up in a kind of intricate psychological dance of thought and feeling. For the subject also this contrasted with his LSD experience, in which he felt much too much in tune with the observers and too subject to a snowballing effect of their mutual interaction into, for example, a paranoid or an intensely sentimental interchange.

The second area of impoverishment was the *inability of the subject*, as noted by the observer, *to identify* with anyone who was not like himself. Thus, in a psychological test involving inspection of photographs of people, the subject could accept and consider only those who were closely like himself—that is, young men. Even there, his associations were sparse, but pictures of children, young women, and older people were totally rejected. This contrasts sharply with the *widening* of associations that we and others noted with LSD and that has been observed with similar drugs.

The third area of impoverishment was *visual perception*. In retrospect, the subject had the conviction that his perception had been subtly altered to a restricted mode that might best be characterized as similar to a cartoon style, as in "Little Orphan Annie." Its characteristics are a stiltedness and plainness of what is perceived—flat, simple, homogeneous areas, sharp, straight margins, and a lack of fineness of detail and texture.

Finally, for several hours after the acute effects of the drug had worn off, Gaarder felt withdrawn and apathetic and experienced a hangover, as is reported in the literature. In so doing, he felt he gained some insight into the physiological nature of hangovers in general. His mild headache seemed to get worse if noises increased or if someone attempted to talk with him. He began to understand a hangover as an acute hypersensitivity to stimuli, so that headache and a wish to withdraw were the primary reactions to relative overstimulation. This is comparable to the observations of Gottlieb's group (Luby et al., 1959) that a person taking Sernyl feels relative tranquility in isolation and irritability in an unrestricted environment.

In summary, we observed that the Sernyl experience differed from the LSD experience in the following ways: instead of marked body-image distortions, there was body-image amnesia; interpersonal sensitivity seemed to diminish; the capacity to identify also seemed to attenuate; the mode of perception seemed to change into one lacking richness of detail; and the hangover following Sernyl seemed to be based on hypersensitivity to stimuli.

After our Sernyl experience, we reported hopefully that psychotomimetic drugs might have a great practical use in creating a specific chemical stress that forces a shift of ego cathexis. They could provide a situation in which the subject and the therapist-observer could deduce which interactions enhance ego control and adaptive mastery and which interactions thwart it. In other words, they offered the potential of a laboratory for the experimental study of the psychotherapy of the psychoses. National recognition of the dangers of such substances, however, soon ended such experimental work.

Our excursion into drug experiences illustrates rather dramatically different possibilities of organizing reality. Particularly striking is the contrast between the expansion into multidimensionality provided by LSD and the narrowing that resulted from Sernyl. A vivid example is the loss of meaning apparent in the verbatim conversation recorded when the subject was under the influence of Sernyl. We observed that a fractionation of temporal experience, the loss of continuity connected to the dramatic diminution of short-term memory, washes out meaning. An individual with temporal disorientation—for example, Kurt Vonnegut's Billy Pilgrim, to whom I referred earlier—may be in "a constant state of stage fright . . . because he never knows what part of his life he is going to have to act in next," but at least he can still act. The loss of meaning connected with the fracture of extremely short time frames, the loss of meaning of what is perceived, makes acting impossible.

The study of psychedelic drug experiences and psychoanalytic clinical material suggested to me a hypothesis linking synesthetic phenomena to a temporal phenomenon, the déjà vu or, more generally, the "déjà" experience introduced in the previous chapter.

Clinical Use of Synesthesia

As in the discussion of LSD, I will be using an extended concept of synesthesia, including not only the blending of sensory compartments—vision, hearing, and so forth—but mood, emotion, space, and time as well. I will illustrate the state by describing in greater detail a patient mentioned briefly in chapter 2.

Anna was an attractive woman in her early thirties, a wife and mother of superior intelligence and advanced academic education. The symptom leading to her referral for psychoanalysis was a fugue state—the most marked of several such episodes—lasting several hours, during which she was in the recreation room of her home with her children, apparently functioning appropriately but unable to recall her actions later. The period was filled with déjà vu sensations and was experienced as uncanny and frightening. During it she experienced fragmented dream images having to do with operations and giant surgeons. Her symptoms also included phobias regarding driving a car and answering telephones and long-standing preoccupations with possibilities of disaster. The phobias had emerged gradually over a number of years but had become more pronounced during the previous three years, after her husband's brief hospitalization for an unconfirmed coronary occlusion.

In the course of psychoanalysis lasting several years, the meaning of the dreamlike images of the fugue states became understandable. The patient had grown up in a small French Canadian town in which her father's family was prominent. Her mother had been reared in an orphanage, and her background had been extremely deprived. Although the patient's father had some scientific training, he only operated a small appliance repair shop and never became financially or otherwise fully independent of his parental family. During the mother's pregnancy with the patient, her two-year-old son died of a renal disease. The patient was thus the only child of a mother who was grieving and chronically depressed. The patient herself had recurrent episodes of pyelitis with high fevers during her childhood.

The patient often experienced the home atmosphere as oppressive. Somewhat masklike smiles, parental—especially maternal—interest in what the patient called "peace-of-mind literature," and the mother's description of her own deprived childhood reinforced the patient's fear of disaster and loss, and also contributed to feelings of guilt. Premature demands were often made of her. For example, when she asked her mother what she should do about bullies who threw stones at her on the way to school, her mother answered blandly that she should search her conscience, where she would find the right thing to do. The patient had also felt reproached when "things came easy"—when, for example, she did well in her studies with little effort.

As the only surviving child, the patient could powerfully influence the mood of her parents, who were fairly isolated socially; thus she began to develop and maintain feelings of omnipotence. She saw her father, who "could make any toy with his hands," as omnipotent until her early adolescence, and her identification with him was strong in many areas. Gradually, however, the patient had recognized the extent of her father's inadequacy and dependence on his own parents. On this basis she had formed some derogatory opinions of men.

When she left home at eighteen to go to college—the same one her father had attended—she intended to be "a better man than Father" and experienced leaving home as liberation. But soon after, her father suddenly died. The patient had made light of her father's anxiety—expressed in his letters to her—about anticipated gall-bladder surgery. He died on the operating table, apparently because heart disease had been misdiagnosed as gall-bladder disease. The patient developed a strong fear of her destructive powers, especially when her omnipotence functioned in the service of competition, and she began to feel that it was dangerous to be liberated from oppressive feelings, dangerous to take matters lightly, and even more dangerous not to anticipate disaster. The dreamlike fragments of the fugue state related to her father's death, the patient identifying both with the destructive surgeons and with the victim suffering retaliation for destructive wishes. The fugue episode had occurred when hostile and competitive feelings toward her husband and resentment about her feminine and maternal role were particularly marked.

As the patient's history unfolded, she was able to see connections between many previously dissociated and isolated areas. Experiencing a sense of continuity between dream material, dreamlike elements of the fugue states, and remembered events and feelings was surprising to her and offered relief.

Although the analysis, of course, involved transference distortions and their interpretation, I would like to focus on one particular aspect of this case: advance in understanding occurred during what might be described as minor repetitions of the so-called fugue states during psychoanalytic hours. In these hours, characterized by a somewhat trancelike atmosphere, references to ongoing experiences of synesthesia were prominent. A shiny object in the office, for instance, would be experienced and described as a "shrill [sounding] object." At this point the patient would report a déjà vu experience and frequently would comment about the uncanniness or awesomeness of the moment. After several minutes of "heavy" silence, an early memory of the "atmosphere"—that is, a synesthetic blending of the sounds, sights, rhythms, tastes, and smells of a certain place or time—would emerge. (The atmosphere of the father's shop was experienced with particular vividness.) A fragmented image from a fugue episode could then be traced to either a fact or a fantasy associated with the time or place characterized by the remembered "atmosphere."

In chapter 2, to clarify the association of synesthetic and déjà vu phenomena in cases of this kind, I drew a schematic analogy with a wave pattern on an oscilloscope representing visual, auditory, or tactile stimuli. I pointed out that a responding organism or electronic scanning machine can be asked if a record is a familiar *visual* pattern, but that if the response is to the *pattern*—regardless of whether the sensory modality is visual, auditory, or tactile—the likelihood that it will be familiar is much increased. In other words, if a pattern of stimulation occurs at a time when the sensory compartments are particularly interwoven or blended, the chances that the pattern will arouse a feeling of familiarity—that is, a déjà vu or related sensation—are multiplied.

Arlow (1959) reviewed much of the literature on déjà vu phenomena and made a major original contribution to the understanding of these experiences. Freud's early view, as summarized by Arlow, was that the déjà vu experience corresponded to the activation of an unconscious impression. Freud came to think, however, that an unconscious fantasy might be involved and not necessarily an unconscious impression of an actual event. Arlow also summarized later extensions of the concept by Ferenczi and Oberndorf, among others, to the effect that not only unconscious fantasies but also repressed fragments of past dreams and consciously experienced intentions that were subsequently repressed may play a part in déjà vu phenomena. Arlow stressed Oberndorf's emphasis on the reassuring quality of the déjà vu experience ("You've been through this before and will come out all right again this time") and also Marcovitz's emphasis of the déjà vu reaction as an expression of the wish to have a second chance. Arlow's original contribution was his formulation, supported by detailed psychoanalytic observations, that the déjà vu reaction contains in its *formal* structure latent elements of defensive reactions and wish-fulfillment. He treated the déjà vu experience reported to him as he would the manifest content of a dream. The person having a déjà vu experience feels that the actual, the manifest situation has occurred previously, whereas it may be that it is not the situation that is familiar but the latent meaning behind it.

Arlow criticized previous formulations for making no attempt to "account for the uncanny, disconcerting, unpleasant, anxiety-tinged affects which usually accompany this form of experience" (p. 614). He added that "the lingering sense of uneasiness or the uncanny which characterizes déjà vu appears to be in proportion to the underlying anxiety and indicates that the ego has not fully succeeded, through the various mechanisms already mentioned, in mastering this anxiety" (p. 629).

Arlow seems to relate the particular uncanny affect to the ambiguity arising from a sense that a manifest situation has occurred previously and at the same time a sense that only the latent meaning of the situation is familiar. The ambiguity here involves several levels of abstraction, since *manifest* and *latent* imply different levels of abstraction, and thus embodies the kind of paradox that I discussed in detail in chapter 2. The ambiguity and uncanniness of the déjà vu experience help establish important conceptual links between time experience (in this case an experience of temporal dislocation) and perception (in this case synesthetic perception). This is a step on the road to my formulations on the mind-time synthesis.

In his paper "Fausse Reconnaissance in Treatment," Freud says, "At the close of a treatment . . . the patient may say: '*Now I feel as though I had known it all the time.*' With this the work of analysis has been completed" (1914, p. 207; Freud's italics). In the analysis of Anna, my déjà vu patient, I believe that there was rapprochement in terms of the schemata of the knowledge of childhood and the schemata of the knowledge of the adult—that is, synesthetic aspects of the childhood schemata were reactivated. The uncanny quality, experiences related to depersonalization, I see as related to premature demands for unambiguous ego functioning. I am here returning to my ideas of analysis as a process of learning to be less uncomfortable with feelings of estrangement from one's own self-experience and perception of the world, from consensually validated reality, a process that leads to tolerance or acceptance of such feelings. I want to emphasize here the word *premature*. As I will elaborate in chapter 4, perceptual processes themselves can undergo maturation, and in mature perceptual acts one can observe the recapitulation of the ontogeny of perception. Clinical data supporting my hypothesis of the pathogenicity of premature demands, including perceptual demands, will also be presented in the following chapter.

Let us now turn from a clinical preoccupation with ambiguity, paradox, and the temporal dislocation of déjà vu phenomena based on synesthetic perception to some of the theoretical themes introduced earlier. Perhaps Gödel has given us a formal logical description of the unconscious by picturing an infinitely regressing series of ambiguities of type. It is in the possibility that these ambiguities must continuously be tapped in order to promote individuation, creativity, and therapeutic work that I see a further link to a psychoanalytic consideration of the problem of the experience of time.

As indicated, the psychoanalyst's major concern with the experience of time is based on his ongoing observation of the restructuring in the present of past experiences. He is in a position to observe the effects of such restructuring on the experience of time and on temporal perspective. Related to the more general problem of paradoxical experience is the issue of integration of the discontinuous moment and the flow of continuity. This issue, which is the ego's task, can be more accurately described as the problem of toleration of qualitatively different, unreconciled paradoxical experiences.

Bonaparte (1940) refers to a communication sent to her by Freud in which he talked of analysts' "later" transformation into continuity of "successive cathexes . . . quanta issuing from the ego." Since, when psychoanalysts speak of the nature of the experience of time, the very word *later* begs the question, I believe that the problem of integration of the discontinuous moment and the flow of continuity was neither avoided nor solved by Freud. The term *quanta*, however, with its implications of the irreconcilable nature—within one closed system—of wave and particle theory, may be of special interest. Freud wrote during the period in which quantum mechanics was being formulated. Quantum mechanics was developed primarily between 1900 and 1926; Heisenberg's uncertainty principle was formulated in 1927; and at the same time physicists began to warn against irresponsible philosophizing and psychologizing based on it. I shall nevertheless attempt some psychologizing, since self-observation of psychic processes confronts us with the static-fluid connotations of the observer-observed situation and, I believe, with its paradoxical implications, related to the different levels of abstraction. An analogy is suggested between the particle and the wave, on the one hand, and the experience of the discontinuous moment and the flow of continuity, on the other. Self-observation attempts to bring together the static grasping the changing grasping the static—opposites on different levels of abstraction; these opposites can be seen as paradoxes—Gödel's infinitely regressing series of ambiguities of type, which I borrowed to serve as a formal logical description of the unconscious.

In a powerful and beautiful paper that considers the *now*-active presence of past and future, Loewald arrives at the concluding formulation that "psychic structures are temporal in nature" (1962, p. 268), that the very fiber of mind is time. I wonder if the temporally conceived form of the paradox of the static and the fluid is not an especially poignant statement, or perhaps the extreme formal statement, of the problem analysts meet at the limits of the study of "what we call psychical" (Loewald, p. 268). William Fry, who says, "Whenever man seeks to inspect the self, he will confront the self and discover that the self is the inspector," also states, "I have . . . discovered no technique of illustrating the *instantaneous* simultaneity created in paradox" (1968, p. 172; italics mine).

In a philosophical tour de force, which it amuses him to entitle paradoxically "A *New* Refutation of Time," Jorge Luis Borges (1964; italics mine) also brings home the extent to which we experience time as the core of the psyche. Not only does he point out how even the idealist philosophers could not follow their own logic to the invalidation of time—which Borges proceeds to do—but he also jars us with his unusual conceptual integration of an experience that seems to have at least some of the features of the déjà vu experience. "That pure representation of homogeneous objects . . . is not merely identical to the one present on that corner so many years ago; it is, *without resemblances or repetitions, the very same*. . . . I felt dead . . . an abstract spectator . . . the possessor of a reticent or absent sense of the inconceivable word eternity. . . . Time . . . is a delusion" (p. 226; italics mine). Similar experiences, usually less explicitly conceptualized, are not unknown in psychoanalytic work, and when they occur, they may represent nodal points of reorganization of life perspective.

Once again, even if the term *object constancy* is restricted to a specific psychoanalytic meaning (continuing investment in an object even though that object may be a frustrating one), the concept cannot be disconnected from continuity in time. The paradox we encounter at the core of time experience—the flowing and the saccadic—is inherent in the problem of object constancy. In considering this paradox and the continuing concern with tolerance of paradoxical and *qualitatively* different experiences, we may perhaps turn with profit to the ego's more obvious task of integrating *quantitatively* different and variable experiences of duration. If we apply the subjective-equivalence concept to time itself, we recall that different clock-time intervals can be experienced as subjectively equivalent. Just as subjectively equivalent object constancies, the building blocks of psychological realities, do not correspond to "objective" constancies, so subjectively equivalent time constancies do not necessarily correspond to "objectively" equivalent *clock-time* intervals.

The concept of subjective equivalence as it applies to time adds another difficult dimension to an already difficult notion that does violence to "common sense." Reality based on subjectively equivalent objects does not take for granted a simple psychological mirroring of external reality. The basic elements of psychological reality are constructs. They are always only more or less stable constructs since the perceptual processes that play a part in "cognitive" formulations are imbedded in an affective matrix. This matrix is dependent on the activity of drives that at any one moment determine the characteristics of one's perceptual scanning. Further, such spatially conceived scanning occurs in a field in which the temporal units have no "externally" given "objective" stability, since objectively identical intervals are not necessarily "subjectively equivalent." An old and extensive literature, dating from the early period of experimental psychology, deals with the search for an irreducible "now," a temporal unit that is the smallest human "present." (In these experiments, "now" is the smallest interval that is neither overestimated nor underestimated.) Whether or not the psychological "packages" of now that I am proposing are the smallest, the irreducible ones, the organization of subjective time depends on complex ongoing equivalence operations, affectively influenced and corrected and modified by fluid adjustments dependent on evaluation of new data and constantly restructured memories.

To restate my difficult proposition: In examining the paradoxical aspects of temporal structure, one can see that embedded in the temporal framework—the temporal mesh—are subjective equivalence patterns. In terms of both the psychoanalytic and the general psychological meaning of object constancy—the idea of an *enduring* object—the object seems to emerge and disappear as the time span and time patterns change; the object varies its guise ambiguously as it moves between paradoxical roles, recurrently producing subjectively equivalent stimuli, the building blocks of both momentary and more lasting realities. Conversely, our needs and drives largely determine on which characteristics of the stimulus field we focus in order to form our subjective equivalences. In changing stimulus fields the time span necessary to locate characteristics that lend themselves to perceptions congruent with the current active drive state must itself continually expand and contract. Our drive states thus determine the subjectively equivalent time spans that anchor our temporal world.

Consider in this context the proposition that each perceptual act recapitulates the history of our perceptual development, a hypothesis supported by recent findings (see chapter 5). Our "realities" then depend on an enormously complex time grid of perception. First, I visualize different sizes of "holes in the grid"—the psychological "nows" determined by the drive states; then, it seems to me, the momentarily active, developmental progression or regression adds different "shapes" or, better, different "textural qualities" to the mesh. Different meshes, to carry the analogy further, permit the passage of different ego states in which object representations have different qualities—as was the case for my patient with the fugue states and the déjà vu experiences. The degree to which synesthetic or sense-compartmentalized perceptual processes characterize each moment is one of the elements in constant flux. The nature of temporal graining—that is, the patterns and textures of the available grids—contributes to the organization of the flow of experience into object constancies. Some drug-induced ego states permit the exploration of extremes of perceptual widening or contraction, perhaps quantitatively but not qualitatively different from what we psychoanalysts encounter in the study of "normal" perception and in clinical work. In one sense our world has been destabilized, but not so in another sense since we have defined some dimensions of the expansions and contractions of this world.

Beyond the clinical enrichment inherent in the analyst's responsiveness to the patient's multiple and paradoxical realities, the study of time leads us to reach hesitantly for the limits of understanding. The basic relationship expounded here is congruent not only with Loewald's statement, "Psychic structures are temporal in nature" (1962, p. 264), but even with the conclusion, mind is time.

Chapter 4

How Do We Change? Diagnostics, Treatments, and "Animation"

It is my intention here to apply the notions of multiple-reality organizations to diagnostic and therapeutic thinking. No systematic survey of current, past, and evolving diagnostic fashions is intended, nor will I attempt a systematic presentation of analytic and therapeutic techniques related to a diagnostic scheme. The wish to establish diagnostic categories that are at least relatively uncontaminated by theoretical preconceptions has led some psychiatrists to formulate diagnostic categories linked relatively closely to observable behaviors (as in the American Psychiatric Association's *DSM-III*, 1980). One area in which behaviors can be observed, however, is the response to various therapeutic interventions, which are of course based on different theoretical models. Diagnostic thinking and therapeutic thinking are intertwined, and both are involved with the pendulum swings between theory building and observation. The ease of or resistance against shifting between different internal reality organizations does have its countertransference dimension, which manifests itself in variations of the therapist's sense of effort and fluctuations in his fatigue. Diagnostic labels are not independent of countertransference. It is therefore appropriate that diagnostic and therapeutic considerations are intertwined in the case material presented below.

For me, the pendulum swings between clinical observation and theory building have led not only to a focus on time in the organization of multiple realities but also to a focus on the boundary between and the differentiation of the animate and inanimate in the construction of psychic realities. The animate-inanimate issue emerged when, after several decades of psychoanalytic practice, I looked for common elements in the patients who seemed to have "changed the most" during—and in my opinion because of—psychoanalytic treatment. Although I tried to free myself temporarily from theoretical preoccupations in the search for a central theme, one theoretical question arose immediately: If we select from our case material the analysands who have "changed the most," are we speaking of those who have experienced "structural" change? What do we understand by this term, and is there a connection between structural alteration and the step from insight to "active" or behavioral change?

Even in a psychoanalytic context, the term *structure* is used in different ways, but here I wish to focus on its meaning in the framework of structural theory—the change, for instance, from a harsh to a more benign superego, or more generally changes within the structures of the mental apparatus or in the relationship between the "structures" of ego, superego, and id.

Loewald discusses structural change in psychoanalytic treatment in the following terms: "If structural change in the patient's personality means anything, it must mean that we assume that ego-development is resumed in the therapeutic process in psychoanalysis" (1960, p. 16). For Loewald the analyst is a *new* object in the patient's life. He thinks of the analyst as a sculptor, but I would emphasize that the sculptor's vision of the finished statue must be influenced by the characteristics of the marble. He frees the form that he sees as kept captive by the stone. Since, as I have spelled out in previous chapters, spatial analogies carry with them dangers of reification, I prefer time-based analogies and would thus prefer the analogy of the creation of a symphony to that of a sculpture. David Rapaport's notion (1960) that structure and function differ only in their respective rates of change is pertinent here.

Loewald's emphasis on a cooperative venture leading to the formation of a *new* structure does offer a framework for clinically derived data about the patients who have "changed the most," and his formulation of structural change remains applicable: "The interpretation takes with the patient the step towards true regression, as against the neurotic compromise formation, thus clarifying for the patient his true regression-level which has been . . . made unrecognizable by . . . defensive . . . structures. . . . by this very step it mediates to the patient the higher integrative level to be reached." The possibility for freer interplay between the unconscious and preconscious systems is thus created by the interpretation. The analytic process then consists of certain integrative experiences between patient and analyst as the foundation for the internalized version of such experiences: reorganization of ego, "structural change" (1960, p. 25).

Rangell (1981) has tried to understand psychoanalytically the difference between patients whose response to insight is "So what?" or "I see this, but what shall I do now?" (p. 131) and those who move autonomously from insight to the initiation of change. Rangell refers to Waelder's statement that analysis offers patients "a possibility of working out a viable, non-neurotic, solution" (p. 135), but the limits of current formulations of the difference between those who act and those who only understand are illustrated by Rangell's need to include unspecified constitutional factors in the formation of more or less action-prone "executive egos."

Although infant observation yields data on variables that could be thought of as constitutional precursors of such characteristics, my observations of adult patients have led me to additional ideas about the more or less "action-prone" features of analysands' "executive egos." I refer to the marked differences between individuals whose behavior does or does not illustrate their experience of themselves as originating centers of autonomous action, either generally or in specific conflictual situations. I tend to think of patients as having undergone "structural changes" to the extent to which changes in the quantities and loci of self-experiences of possible autonomous action have occurred. Those in whom such changes have taken place may or may not *choose* to make certain changes in their lives, but any lack of action is for them deliberate and not the result of inhibition. Discussions with colleagues have revealed that when they think of patients who have experienced "structural change" their clinical understanding of the term approximates mine.

A retrospective view of cases in which significant change, perhaps structural change, had occurred led me to the observation that they were characterized by a change in focus from animate to inanimate features of "objects" encountered in the analytic work. This observation would be banal if it were simply a description, in slightly different words, of dead issues becoming live issues and vice versa. The form in which certain life-or-death issues were encountered in some of these analyses—specifically, brief but important *perceptions* of animate objects as inanimate—suggested the possibility that aspects of the experience might hark back to the infant's dawning awareness of the differentiation of the inanimate and animate worlds. In other words, the question arose of whether the analysand's experiences of objects changing, on a symbolic level, from animate to inanimate and vice versa—a change in the *relationship to objects*—might be connected to the perceptual discrimination between the animate and the inanimate, and even to the infant's development of this differentiation. If, indeed, the readiness for such shifts in cathexis to *symbolic* representations of the animate and inanimate depends on the individual's history of *perceptual* experiences (even if the perceptual animate-inanimate switch is clear and explicit only in some cases), awareness of such a relationship could lead to a better understanding of the development of action-prone executive egos.

In musing further about animate-inanimate discrimination as an early developmental task, I conceived of it as probably intimately connected to but not identical with the inner-outer discrimination. It is a discrimination necessary for action: the animate reacts. Nevertheless, this early discrimination is, paradoxically, not a very firm one. Does our anxiety about dying spur us to animate the universe as we do, so that we perceive living clouds and the embracing rays of the sun? At any rate, interweaving with temporal and other ambiguities, the animate-inanimate problem endures, finding expression in subtle and usually unnoticed ways that may be ego-syntonic additions to defensive maneuvers against death. In listening to their patients, analysts may unconsciously compensate for animate-inanimate slips just as they often do for other kinds of slips until they train themselves to special alertness.

Once I became aware of the possible significance of changes in animate-inanimate discrimination in clinical material, my own defensive not-hearing—my compensating for patients' slips indicating their confusion between the animate and inanimate realms— diminished. I discovered how prevalent such confusion was in the productions of many of my patients. Different features of change in the animate-inanimate discrimination characterized different patient groups, however. These variations were diagnostically important and were related to the severity of the pathology. Changes in animate-inanimate discrimination occur in, and can direct the analyst to, *discrete* conflict areas in neurotic patients. A structural alteration in this discriminatory function has occurred in these patients, and psychoanalytic work can bring about a corrective structural change. Derivatives of *widespread* confusion of the animate and inanimate realms run through most of the clinical work with borderline and narcissistic patients. This pervasiveness, I believe, accounts for some of the difficulties of obtaining structural change in such patients. In psychotic patients, animate-inanimate confusion is *massive and pervasive*. The manifestations of the problem in these patients can be subtle, however, because this confusion is so intertwined with other boundary problems. With the usual reservations about the unavoidable oversimplifications and incompleteness of summaries of the work of many years, I will now turn to clinical material, going from less to more severe psychopathology.

Clinical Illustrations

Mrs. A, forty years old, married since her early twenties, and mother of four boys, had been greatly concerned about her husband's health. Her anxiety was apparently somewhat contagious both to Mr. A and to some of his physicians: Mr. A was hospitalized twice for diagnostic workups, but they resulted in a clean bill of health. In addition, marital dissatisfaction of recent origin had led Mr. and Mrs. A to seek couple therapy at her

initiative. Apparently she had been finding him much more aggressive and sarcastic than previously, and he had been experiencing her as more anxious, provocative, and critical. When the
mutual accusatory pattern did not yield to treatment and the marital
tension continued to increase, the therapist recommended individual treatment for both. According to Mrs. A, her husband had
become vehemently opposed to the idea of any treatment for any-
body, but by this time her growing depression and interpersonal
difficulties with her sons and many of her friends led her to seek
more consultations. Eventually she decided to enter psychoanalysis, during which the following story emerged.

Mrs. A was the youngest of a large number of children, all
girls. When she was between four and five years old, a brother was
born, but he died at the age of two. Mrs. A became an attractive
adolescent and young woman; she had many boyfriends, whom
she usually brought home to meet her family. The young man who
later became her husband was studying the same narrow sub-
specialty of the technical field in which her father worked. Of all
the young men she brought home, he was the only one with whom
her father had lengthy conversations and developed a genuine
relationship—a relationship that continued to flourish after the
marriage. Mr. A's career prospered, and the couple's four sons
developed well. For many years Mrs. A seeemed to experience no
dissatisfaction with her life—or at least she gave no *signs* of
dissatisfaction.

Her concern for her husband's health and the complaints and
symptoms that led to couple therapy and then to her entering
analysis occurred a few months after her father's death. This
information, I might add, was somewhat slow in emerging because of a sequence of "errors" made by Mrs. A in giving and
elaborating on her history. Eventually, however, she described
how one morning, not long after her father's death, she had looked
critically at her sleeping husband, had experienced him briefly as a
stranger, and then had the thought, "What am I doing—being
married to *that*?" She later elaborated that, for a brief moment, she
had experienced him as dead—"like a piece of wood."

It will come as no surprise to a psychoanalyst reading this story
that the following understanding emerged from psychoanalytic

work: Mrs. A had had death wishes for her younger male sibling, who had been greatly desired by the family, especially her father. The inevitable psychoanalytic formulation involved her guilt feelings connected to her brother's death, the replacement or restitution motive in her marital choice, the centrality in her emotional life of her relationship to her father, for whom she also produced and raised her four sons, and finally the collapse of the essential meaning of her life with her father's death. The problems that had brought Mrs. A to therapy reflected the degree of resistance and the complexity of the maneuvers she had employed to avoid facing her emotional bankruptcy after her father died. When her husband was no longer serving a bridging function to her father, she began to recognize, at some level, that he was an inappropriate mate, a genuinely poor choice. Eventually she divorced her husband and relatively late in life resumed her education so that she was able to embark on a professional career. The points I wish to develop, however, could be made if the patient had instead discovered that the marriage was more meaningful than ever to her, that she was married to a man with whom she could have a loving relationship now that he no longer had to serve such a concrete bridging function.

Schematically presented, the transference-related *action* in the analysis began to surface around a remark indicating that the patient was hiding the time of her analytic session from her husband. Why? He was a violent man who didn't want her to be in analysis, but she had already told him that she was seeing a psychoanalyst. What would be the effect of his knowing the particular days and times of the sessions? Well, he might just kill her—or (variations on the theme were rapidly played out over several sessions) he might kill the analyst. It became clear that by informing him of the analysis and making a point of being secretive about the days and hours, she was being very provocative. Exploration of the theme of provocation of violence (she might have to kill him in self-defense or in defending the analyst—from an attack on him that she would have provoked) led through dreams and associations to her death wishes directed primarily against her husband and the analyst (in various transferentially determined roles); finally, after corrections and amplification of the history she had previously given, the trail led to affectively charged memories of her brother's death and to the formulation given above.

Affectively charged recall, in a treatment in which a transference neurosis had developed, and insight—in this case leading to specific action—are the concepts used in a psychoanalytic description of change. Had there been structural change? A great part of Mrs. A's life had been organized around her guilt connected to her brother's death. One could say that her psychic reality was that she *had* killed him, a psychic reality reactivated in the heat of the transference and manifesting itself in the various "who would kill whom" scenarios related to her provocative behavior. One could also say that in a sense life had played a cruel joke on Mrs. A. She had unconsciously organized a good portion of her life as if she *had* killed her brother, and psychoanalysis had helped her to change from, escape from, the role of victim by illuminating the "adult" reality that she had *not* killed her brother. Perhaps one could say that she learned in analysis just how much she had wanted to kill her brother, in the context of her derepressing various aspects of her wishes, including sexual ones, for her father. I believe that she learned something about the intensity of her death wish on different developmental levels, and that such learning in turn involved contact with different levels of the development of perception.

Once again the notion that each perceptual act recapitulates the ontogeny of perception is pertinent to a psychoanalytic understanding of object constancy. Such a recapitulation would bring the individual again and again into brief contact with the earliest perceptual processes, and there are indications that the discrimination between the animate and the inanimate is precisely one such process. Some years ago, for instance, Margaret Mahler (personal communication, 1973) called my attention to Stirnimann's 1947 finding that the normal infant's differential grasp shows the ability to discriminate in the first hours of life between a proferred finger, a gloved finger, a glove without a finger, and a stick.

Although insufficient and oversimplified, it is accurate to say that Mrs. A discovered in a situation laden with transference affect that wish and deed were not identical, a differentiation that was not solidly established at the time of her brother's death. Greenspan (1982) has shown that during psychoanalytic treatment different levels of learning are integrated. He speaks of somatic learning, of consequence learning, and of representational-structural learning. Different levels of learning involve different levels of perceptual development—that is, a close connection exists between perceptual recapitulation and the integration of different levels of learning. When Mrs. A admitted to consciousness the thought, "What am I doing—being married to *that*?" the literal meaning was important: *That* was not human. *That* was not animate. *That* was a thing. The frenetic activity that followed, the hypochondriasis *for* her husband, represented efforts to breathe some life into the scene.

The change in Mrs. A's life is easily visible because she *acted*—after acquiring insight—to alter her situation. Despite its importance in the background and its possible emergence at nodal points of change, material related to the animate-inanimate differentiation may not be noticed at all or may not demand focused attention in the analysis of neurotic patients with a *relatively* uncomplicated developmental history of this differentiation. As Loewald (1960, p. 25) puts it, "The analyst in his interpretations reorganizes, reintegrates unconscious material for himself as well as for the patient." I believe that the analyst's ability to be in touch to some extent with the patient's "de-animation" is therapeutically useful in general. Mrs. A, however, like many other patients without major ego deficits, was spurred into action in treatment and then in life not only through a transferentially activated confrontation with her destructive wishes but also through a regressive brief encounter with the uncanny breakdown of the inanimate-animate boundary—when her husband had been transformed into "that." Inasmuch as Mr. A, in a deep sense, had been a quasi-inert instrument of contact with her father, who was the real object of her live cathexis, the experience of her husband as "that" was of course accurate.

The domain of the ambiguity between the animate and the inanimate is the area of the uncanny, which during analytic treatment is briefly encountered by some patients (such as Mrs. A) but which is an area of recurrent or prolonged immersion for other patients. The following example also illustrates a significant en-counter with the animate-inanimate boundary in treatment.

In one session, a brilliant and highly creative young scientist was discussing his doubts about whether or not to marry his girlfriend, the possibility that she might be pregnant, and related issues that could justify a considerable degree of emotional tur-moil. Yet his agitation and at times his bewilderment in the session seemed disconnected from the content. The analyst commented on that impression and inquired about other areas in the patient's life. In response, the patient was flooded with tears and suddenly recalled a dream. He was flying over a beautiful city, which he described in exquisite detail. When he flew lower and lower over the city and searched for signs of life, however, he discovered that it was absolutely dead—no bustling activities downtown, no chil-dren in the schoolyards, no life in the residential areas.

The patient's associations led to his work. In a creative storm—working night and day—he had just solved a fundamental problem, a problem that had been recognized for over a hundred years, about which many books had been written, and about which there had been many lively controversies. He had found a simple and elegant solution to the old problem—he could fly over the city now—but the intense life around a basic scientific question, an area of research and agitation in which he had been a major participant, had come to an abrupt end. The problem was dead. The significance of the patient's achievement (and "achieving," incidentally, also means killing) was soon widely recognized and led to a meteoric rise in his career. His colleagues also commented that his writing style at this point changed radically. Although working in a rigorous and highly abstract scientific field, he was often complimented thereafter about the change from the dry style customary in his field to a remarkably readable, animated style, which conveyed with simple elegance the growth and unfolding of his thought.

Throughout the patient's childhood and youth, his father had engaged him in fierce chess battles, whose competitiveness was closely connected to the patient's subsequent scientific intensity. Rich analytic material illustrated how his scientific breakthrough was related to oedipal issues and his ability to deal with an oedipal victory. This explanatory interpretation, however, does not detract from the significance for him, at the moment of profound change, of contact with the *uncanny* boundary of the lifeless, perhaps with the structural difference of the animate and inanimate.

Freud discusses such an encounter primarily in his cultural and anthropological works, although these interests are, of course, not segregated for him from clinical concerns. The topic is a central one in his paper "The 'Uncanny' " (1919), but in *Totem and Taboo* (1913) he had already touched on the connection of the uncanny experience with the animate-inanimate boundary: "We appear to attribute an 'uncanny' quality to impressions that seek to confirm the omnipotence of thoughts and the animistic mode of thinking in general, after we have reached a stage at which, in our *judgment,* we have abandoned such beliefs" (*S.E.,* 13:86).

In my psychoanalytic work with Anna, the hysterical patient discussed in chapters 2 and 3 whose presenting difficulties included fugue states and who had many déjà vu experiences during analytic sessions, I noticed a pseudoanimism, a peculiar aliveness of objects in the analyst's office, which characterized these states. The episodes proved to be defensive against the reliving of a particularly unexpected encounter with death in a situation when she had made light of potential danger. Here, the animate-inanimate issue was important in work with a neurotic, basically hysterical patient, and the prevalence of synesthetic and déjà vu phenomena seemed to contribute to the (pseudo)-animism. I will return later to the association between synesthesia, déjà vu experiences, uncanniness, and a fluid animate-inanimate boundary.

The animate-inanimate problem appears perhaps most frequently and typically in analysis and psychoanalytic psychotherapy in the work with patients with pronounced narcissistic traits. Because my ideas about the importance of the problem also have more direct consequences for therapeutic technique with such patients, I will emphasize technical considerations in illustrating the animate-inanimate issue in narcissistic patients.

A young divorcée started her Monday morning hour with a barrage of complaints centering on her inability to cope with a baby who cried at all hours of the night and a boyfriend in whom she was more interested than he was in her. In her account there was no differentiation in the tone she used to describe things that *happened to her* and things she *did*. She continued to complain about her own bad driving, her overeating, and her wish to kill her baby. The whole picture was presented as an attack on the analyst, who she said had not helped her with any of her problems. She continued, "It is not safe for me to drive. I have had some vague thoughts of killing myself, and the car seems to agree with me. Wouldn't start."

Some clinicians refer to the behavior features in this brief sketch as "entitlement"—a person's failure to differentiate between events that result from volitional action (consciously or unconsciously volitional) and external events, those that are not immediately related to identifiable intentionality. The analyst's problem in such situations concerns the ego syntonicity for the patient of such lack of differentiation—that is, the analyst must explore why it seems so natural to the patient not to differentiate between such complaints as eating too much, a car that won't start, and a thunderstorm. In his later work *Search for a Method* (1960), which has largely been ignored by psychoanalysts, Jean-Paul Sartre emphasized the distinction between *praxis* (actions resulting from intentionality) and *process* (processes related to inert matter). I believe that if therapeutic efforts with patients such as the one I am describing are successful, an important area of change is the patient's ability to differentiate between the results of praxis, on the one hand, and of inert processes or the haphazard, on the other.

A close look at the exchanges in the analytic session may illustrate a direct technical application of some of the ideas developed here. Because her car wouldn't start, my patient took a taxi. Because a friend of hers had recently been mugged, she experienced acute anxiety when the driver took her over an unfamiliar route and through a part of the city where there were few people on the street. At the time of this session, several years into the analysis, the analyst had already learned that it was unproductive for him to confront her with her propensity to treat events that she had caused in the same manner as externally caused events. Instead, the analyst asked if she had thought about the mugging while in the cab. The patient replied that she had indeed and that she had also thought about murders she had read about in the newspaper. The analyst's next intervention was based on the idea that the danger in the atmosphere, so to speak, should be addressed rather than the location of the source of the danger, because he saw the patient's difficulties as being rooted in an uncompleted differentiation of who or what can initiate action—that is, ultimately, of what is animate—from what is acted upon, the inanimate. Carefully choosing his words, the analyst said: "You have been in touch with a lot of murderous feelings since our last session. You had murderous feelings against your baby, and you had thoughts about murderous feelings directed against you." Again, what was important, I believe, was the analyst's *not* confronting the patient with the analyst's own differentiation of praxis and process, the actor and the acted upon, but rather watching carefully over the development of that differentiation in the patient. (Note also, however, the analyst's differentiation of "feelings," on the one hand, and "thoughts about feelings," on the other.) It does not advance the work if the analyst, feeling unfairly accused and held responsible for everything that goes wrong in the patient's life, responds—or, perhaps more accurately, retaliates—with confrontation, in effect saying that the patient *should* be big enough to differentiate between what she is doing and what happens to her.

How, then, can change occur in such an analytic situation? A few months after the session described above, the patient again spoke of a series of unfortunate developments in her life. She had had a bad night. For various reasons the analyst believed that the patient was not reporting a dream. He asked, "In this terrible night, did you have any dreams?" The patient became restless and said, "Yes, but I can't remember." The restlessness continued and after a fairly long pause the patient said, "Well, there were people, and I was literally coming apart. The buttons on my blouse wouldn't stay closed." "Too many demands pulling you apart," the analyst said. "But it's not exactly like that," the patient continued. "There was something sloppy about it. Self-demeaning. I'm getting fat." Note that the patient was not attacking the analyst and did not blame him for her overeating. There were some indications of embarrassment. She used the neutral way of phrasing that had been characteristic of the analyst's way of commenting: "There was something sloppy about it." She moved to "self-demeaning," which was followed by "I'm getting fat." She was en route to the autonomous experience that she was eating too much and that she could initiate eating less. The patient proved to be en route to more autonomous experience generally.

Strachey's (1934) notions about change, identifications with the analyst, and the taking in of small doses of reality about the analyst are relevant here, along with Loewald's emphasis on the analyst's facilitating true regression and thus a new beginning, with its consequent distancing from current compromise formation. For the present purposes, however, I would like to emphasize that the analyst's technique was informed by the notion that the patient's difficulty was related to a problem in the development of perceptual differentiation. Confrontation was avoided. This made unnecessary the compromise formations that were the patient's usual response to the attacks her behavior elicited. The vicious cycle was broken. In Loewald's language, a true regression—to a state in which the animate and the inanimate were not adequately differentiated—made possible a new beginning. "Process," in Sartre's language, was gradually changed to "praxis."

Let me elaborate: the patient said she "wanted" to come to her analytic session and thought that the stalling engine was a process phenomenon, the fault of inert matter. Suppose, however, that in analysis it became clear that her neglect of her car was related to the ambivalence she harbored vis-à-vis her treatment. Then the *process* would have been changed to *praxis*. In such an analytic situation inroads on the preconscious can transform much that is "accidental" into meaningful sequence. Slips are no longer haphazard, even to the patient. I will return later to some epistemological consequences of the discovery of the uncertainty of the boundary between the meaningful and the haphazard. If we cannot trust the border anymore, is there possible meaning everywhere, or is there meaning nowhere?

Finally, I turn to case material of more severe psychopathology—to Mary, the self-mutilating borderline patient mentioned briefly in chapter 2. Such patients demonstrate in their psychopathology the pervasiveness of issues related to animate-inanimate discrimination. Mary had had a severe skin disorder during the language-learning period, and her later foremost symptomatology included repeatedly cutting her skin, when she experienced herself as inanimate, and then interfering with the wound's healing (Kafka, 1969).

Problems of limits—the limits of her body, the limits of her power, and the limits of her capacity to feel—were of major importance in Mary's analysis. Winnicott's concepts of transitional objects and transitional phenomena (1958a) provide a useful framework for the formulation of some aspects of the patient's history of object relationships. I want to develop the idea that a patient's own body can be treated by her as a transitional object and that this can be related to a history of self-injury. I will also explore some effects of this history of object relationships on the development of transference and countertransference.

When one speaks of transitional objects, the image that most easily evokes a response in the listener is Linus's security blanket in the comic strip "Peanuts." Mary illuminated for me an expanded way of thinking about possible transitional objects. One can approach this point of view by visualizing the initial frames of the films used to teach surgery to medical students. A piece of carefully cleansed skin is shown, surrounded by nonreflecting blue drapes; the location of the skin is explained in the accompanying technical commentary; and then the surgeon's gloved hand makes a rapid scalpel incision. There is a pause, which the viewer experiences as longer than it is, before blood wells up—before the viewer experiences the emotional shift from what seems inanimate surgical anatomy to confrontation with the wound. I am proposing that the self-mutilator again and again treats her own skin and body in a somewhat similar fashion, as if at some point she sees it as inanimate and transitional. In theorizing about such matters we must be careful, of course, to remain aware of the limitation of words, for we are dealing with nonverbal, largely preverbal material. Yet even catchphrases, such as "transitional object," may be useful in producing the contagious atmosphere that enables us to participate in the other person's experience.

Mary was a college student in her late teens when I started working with her. Her psychoanalytic treatment lasted almost five years, during the first two of which she was hospitalized. Her father is a dry, undemonstrative engineer, and her mother is a talkative woman with hysterical and hypochondriacal characteristics. The patient has one older brother, whose superior academic performance she envied. Her parents had been separated for several years prior to her hospitalization. A psychiatrist who had seen Mary on a less intensive basis for over a year had referred her for psychoanalysis in a hospital setting because of symptoms consisting primarily of cutting herself and interfering with wound healing. Sometimes she also swallowed pills indiscriminately, refused to take medications, or cheated in taking medications. She narcissistically considered and treated practically her whole body surface as an almost constant object of erotic fascination.

Interference with wound healing had apparently been present since childhood, probably since the age of six or eight years, but the symptoms, especially cutting, had increased in frequency since her parents' separation. Mary was scarred primarily on her arms, but her appearance was generally pasty and her demeanor listless when I started working with her.

During her first year of life Mary had been gravely ill with a generalized dermatitis diagnosed as an allergic reaction. Problems related to touching and skin sensitivity had thus been prominent since infancy. Furry pets and dolls were always common in the household, and early contacts with these objects were related to the importance of texture for Mary. Mother and daughter competed in taking care of the pets. For years prior to the parents' separation, the father had had a relationship with another woman and had totally neglected his wife sexually. Thus the mother had a strongly eroticized interest in the household pets and also in her particularly cuddly daughter, for whom the atmosphere also became diffusely eroticized. The mother instructed Mary in how to spy on the father, whose infidelity was always suspected. The father, in turn, was aware of his daughter's inquisitiveness. Mary had repetitive self-destructive thoughts and thoughts that she was in danger when she was with him—for example, it would occur to her that he wanted to push her from a bridge—and she had at least brief thoughts of how she might retaliate. Erotic feelings toward her father were thus particularly interwoven with sadomasochistic elements. The mother used a variety of conversion symptoms to

force some attention from her husband and others, and she openly
showed her delight when Mary similarly got her way in a situation
in which that did not seem possible, such as when she somehow
persuaded a bus driver to stop the bus en route so she could get a
soft drink. Her feelings of omnipotence were encouraged in this
and a variety of other ways. For example, from the age of fifteen
on, as a volunteer in an animal care and rescue center, Mary had
the power of life and death over stray animals: she could decide
which were to be put to sleep and which were to be offered for
adoption.

Early phases of the psychoanalytic work were often characterized by Mary's sullen, silent attitude, to which I found myself
responding similarly. After two months of analysis the problem of
the limits of her powers was highlighted dramatically: she developed a fulminating case of viral pneumonia which required transfer to a general hospital. She went rapidly downhill, and despite
heroic measures the internist and consultant expressed the opinion
that she was terminal and would not survive the next forty-eight
hours. When fully conscious in the oxygen tent, she still insisted
that she wanted to drink only a particular kind of fruit juice, not
readily available, and refused the more common juices that were
offered. At this point I told her that she was not expected to survive
and that she might as well drink the available juice if she still
wanted to taste any juice at all. A marked behavioral change
occurred at that time. She looked frightened, talked about her fear
of death, and drank the juice that was offered. This seemed to mark
a clear turning point and left me with the feeling that my ability to
be blunt with her had saved her life. After her recovery from
pneumonia, the theme of my power over her life and death became
a prominent one in analysis. Cutting of her arms and legs continued until I experienced fully my inability to save her life. She
then seemed to experience more power over her own life, and self-
mutilation stopped.

The unfolding of the transference provided most of the history
of her development that I have described. When I sensed an
unusual number of erotic and sadistic fantasies, the work of analysis identified them as representing repressed aspects of both
parents' relationships with Mary, but predominantly the mother's.

In discussing the analysis, I will single out for further description and theoretical consideration her experience of her own body, and my frequent echoing experience of her as not quite living matter. I will not dwell on the more routine psychoanalytic work, but there was much working through of material relating to complexities of interpersonal relationships as she eventually moved out of the hospital, became a private patient, found work, had plastic surgery to remove at least some of her many scars, and started to have increasingly frequent and meaningful dates. The intensive and complex work with Mary's family and the difficult and subtle administrative and nursing management of her hospital stay will also not be described here (but see Burnham, 1966, for a description of how she decorated almost every inch of her room with furry or other textured objects, pictures of animals, and so on).

In proceeding to a description of the heart of Mary's analysis, I return first to Winnicott:

> It is generally acknowledged that a statement of human nature is inadequate when given in terms of interpersonal relationships. There is another way of describing persons . . . that suggests that of every individual who has reached to the stage of being a unit *with a limiting membrane and an outside and an inside* [italics mine] it can be said that there is an *inner* reality to that individual, an inner world which can be rich or poor or can be at peace or in a state of war.
>
> My claim is that if there is a need for this double statement there is a need for a triple one; there is the third part of the life of a human being, a part that we cannot ignore, an intermediate area of *experiencing*, to which inner reality and external life both contribute. It is an area which is *not challenged* [italics mine], because no claim is made on its behalf except as it exists as a resting place for the individual engaged in the perpetual *human* [italics mine] task of keeping inner and outer reality separate yet interrelated. (1958a, p. 230)

Winnicott subtitled this paper "Study of the First *Not Me* Possession," which seems to me to be pertinent to my discussion of Mary, who considered her body in precisely these terms. Early in life she had had spiked braces placed on her teeth in an unsuccessful attempt to keep her from thumbsucking and resultant bad teeth alignment; later she was fascinated by the theme of auto-cannibalism. She had vivid fantasies about starving Arctic explorers eating parts of their own bodies to survive, and at times she actually ate small (and sometimes not so small) pieces of the flesh and skin of her own fingers.

Because of apparently life-threatening early allergic dermatitis, Mary's entire body had been swaddled and bandaged during most of her first year. As mentioned earlier, Winnicott suggests that the pattern of transitional phenomena begins to show somewhere between four and twelve months (1958a, p. 232). Particular care was given to the problem of keeping Mary from irritating her skin with her own hands. The parents also recalled the problems related to picking up and touching the baby and managed to convey a picture of what is likely to have been contact hunger and acute pain with contact.

In the course of the analysis, Mary described her sensations when she slowly and deliberately cut herself—for instance, with a razor blade or with a broken light bulb smuggled under her bed covers—while gazing lovingly at her "favorite nurse," who was "specialing" her. At first she would not feel it, but "I always stopped as soon as I did feel it," and she managed to convey the exquisite border experience of sharply "becoming alive" at that moment. This sharp sensation was then followed by the flow of blood; in her description, the blood seemed like a voluptuous bath, a sensation of pleasant warmth that spread over the hills and valleys of her body, molding its contour and sculpting its form. In speaking of her blood, Mary communicated a relationship with a transitional object—the sense that as long as one has blood, one carries within oneself a potential security blanket capable of giving warmth and comforting envelopment. Dream and fantasy material suggested that *internal* blood was probably linked to the internalized mother and that the patient felt superior to others or omnipotent because *she* could use her knowledge to make this comforting mother-blanket external. Winnicott says that the mother herself can be the transitional object ("Sometimes there is no transitional object except the mother herself"—1958a, p. 232), but he does not specifically make the point being stressed here—

that part of the body (here the blood, representing the internalized mother) can be a transitional object.

Throughout a major portion of the analysis, Mary expressed concern (or threatened) that the pleasurable sensation associated with cutting would make it impossible for her to resist the temptation to scar herself, particularly her face and trunk. At times she not only felt superior to others but seemed genuinely puzzled as to how others could go through life without even occasionally indulging in the forbidden fruit of a blood bath available so readily through a "zip" in the skin. She made jokes about having zippers in the skin and reported many dreams related to shedding of skin, burned tarpaper forming peeling blisters, and so on. She also reported that during her childhood in a northern city, she often had vivid fantasies during frequent snowball fights that an invisible layer around her stopped snowballs at some distance from her body. Such fantasies may have been related to her weight, which had fluctuated greatly during much of her life. She was fascinated by a magazine article describing an avant-garde artist who painted the skin of his models and then instructed them to transfer the pigment to canvas by throwing their bodies on the canvas or rolling themselves against it. For years prior to this, she herself had made designs by letting worms crawl through spilled ink onto white paper. In both techniques, the fascination lay in the use of the living body as a tool, an object transitional between living and dead matter. Worms were of particular interest to Mary for their clearly segmented structure, the fact that excretory and sexual organs were in *each* segment, and their ability to grow parts after they had been severed. (Parenthetically, one may ask if a segment of a worm is a whole or a part-object.) Perhaps it would make sense here to talk of something *transitional* between the part and the whole object.

In the countertransference, when I experienced the patient as not quite living, not quite animate, I too was relating to a transitional object. In retrospect, one of the factors that permitted me to be so blunt, or perhaps so *sharp*, with Mary when she was apparently dying of pneumonia was my experiencing her as a not-quite-living person. The degree to which one ascribes to another the quality of being alive (assuming that one considers oneself alive) depends on the ability to be empathic or to identify with the other person. With her pasty appearance and her ability to slice into her own skin without any change in facial expression, Mary seemed to treat herself as a not quite living object, or at least to consider parts of her body as something other than her own living tissue. My reaction in the face of her self-mutilations was not always "Don't do that! Don't hurt yourself. I won't let you hurt yourself." My experience was perhaps more in line with what Winnicott has called "hate in the countertransference" (1958b); at least my subjective feelings could have been verbalized along the lines of "Go ahead, slice yourself to ribbons; let's find out if you're alive or not."

Earlier I expressed the idea that in order to permit her infant to take a first step, a mother must have the delusion that the infant will not fall, a predifferentiation delusion of unity. Work with Mary was one of the factors that have now led me to believe that another parental delusion, if you will, is necessary to permit individuation of the offspring. The delusion is that the offspring is not alive. Let me explain. It is generally believed that physicians cannot adequately treat members of their own families because they are not "objective" enough. To rephrase this: they cannot treat members of their own families sufficiently as *nonliving objects*. At crucial times, however, every parent *must* be a little bit of a doctor in treating his own offspring. A patient comes to mind, for instance, who was paralyzed in his parental function in the face of his child's slightest injury. There are some moments, borderline situations, in which not only the treatment of children's injuries but also the more general *rearing* of children demands the infliction of pain; however brief such moments may be, as parents we can handle them only if we consider the "tissue" as not quite as alive and responsive as our own.

On the descriptive level, I believe that we are on rather firm ground in applying the transitional-object concept to such a situation. This patient certainly *did* treat parts of the surface of her body as though she were dealing with not-quite-living skin, and there is much evidence to support the notion that she was much preoccupied with what was for her the very much *unfinished business* of establishing her body scheme.[1]

In applying the transitional-object concept to the *genetic* aspects of this case, to the developmental roots in the history of the patient, I feel on somewhat less firm ground. Genetically, I conceptualize the intensity of the early contact hunger, and the pain when there *was* contact, as a traumatic fixation point, an area of still strikingly "unfinished business" when analysis began, an area in which the "perpetual human task of keeping inner and outer reality separate yet interrelated" (Winnicott, 1958a, p. 230) was particularly difficult. The possibility that a dramatic connection probably existed in this case between the early skin disease and the later symptom may offer a lead to other such patients. Early traumatic fixation points relating particularly to the formation of the membrane of the body scheme may play a part in the developmental history of other patients with the cutting syndrome, although less dramatically. The previously developed thesis that benevolent parental communication of tolerance of ambiguity is related to the offspring's individuation without alienation would also find expression here in the ambiguity of hunger for contact and at the same time pain through contact.

Without spelling out again Winnicott's work on the formation of psychic membranes, let us focus on the membrane of particular concern here—the cutter's skin. Although sadism and masochism are usually considered two sides of the same coin, one or the other often dominates a particular clinical picture. The study of how one's own body can be a "not-me" object may illuminate the general question of the sadistic or masochistic preference. In a sense, the cutter's choice is a transitional one between the sadistic and masochistic object, his *own not-me* skin. The skin is his own—but he experiences it as *not* his own. In analysis the ebb and

1. In this context the fine but important distinction between Schilder's body image (1950) and Federn's (1952) notion of a bodily ego feeling may be pertinent. This distinction refers on the one hand to the knowledge of how one's body functions as a tool, as an instrument, and on the other hand to the feeling of emotional intimacy with one's body, its being part of the "me" feeling. It is perhaps in this border area between body image and bodily ego feeling that the transitional-object concept makes the most sense.

flow of sadomasochistic transference and countertransference may be conceptualized as related to the development and vicissitudes of the animate-inanimate differentiation, a factor contributing to the re-formation of a more integrated, more ego-syntonic body membrane and thus to the eventual elimination of the symptom.

As I have illustrated, confusion between animate and inanimate characteristics is present when major conflicts are activated in neurotic patients, and it is more pervasive in borderline and narcissistic patients. I have asserted that it is widespread in schizophrenic phenomenology and that the animate-inanimate problem seems to be near the psychotic—the autistic—core. In his work on the nonhuman environment, Searles (1960) collected much clinical material that is pertinent here. In the following chapter, I will deal specifically with schizophrenia, but in order to maintain the continuity from less severe to more severe pathology, I will offer a brief clinical illustration here.

A young man who had been hospitalized for years with flagrant schizophrenic pathology had apparently made a remarkable recovery. The degree of his insight and his descriptive abilities were considerable. In describing his emergence from psychosis, he characterized his first transitory moment of feeling normal again as "feeling that he was feeling." "Feeling that he was *not* feeling" was his characterization of his abnormal state. At such times, he felt that his surroundings—the walls, cars, rugs, and so forth— were not real, that perhaps they had been put there to fool him, to make him believe that something real *was* there. Even then he had seemed to succeed in believing in his own existence, however, in a kind of "cogito ergo sum." He existed, but there was no possibility of his having any kind of effect on what was around him. There is, he said, no possibility that what exists can have any impact on what does not exist.

I think of such a state as the absence of an *integrated* feeling of oneself as animate, and I believe that projections and projective identifications of nonexistence are involved. The patient's descriptions brought to mind science fiction stories about isolated heads or perhaps brains existing in nutrient solutions. The patient said that what saved his life ("what made me feel alive") was a psychiatric aide's saying to him, "You are somebody; you can do what you want." I do not know what factors were responsible for the patient's ability to *hear* at that particular moment, to experience himself at that particular moment as an autonomous center of action capable of "connecting" with his surroundings, of having an impact on them. When only he existed and the other existences around him were "pretend," he was not psychologically animate. Anima means breath, breathe, animate means movement—or the potential of movement—that connects; in connecting, it establishes whether the other is *inert matter* or another *animate center of autonomous action.*

Discussion

To summarize some of the ideas presented in this chapter, the following hypothesis is clinically derived and seems clinically useful. The animate and the inanimate are "representational structures" that serve as anchors in our organization of ourselves and thus as anchors in the interpersonal network that makes communication possible. Among the earliest perceptual tasks is discrimination of the fundamental structural differences between the animate and the inanimate. The individual's developmental history of perception is the foundation upon which the gradual integration of various levels of learning (somatic, consequential, and representational-structural learning in Greenspan's [1982] Piagetian schema, for instance) is based. Such integration is necessary to avoid the danger of *action* contamination of our *ideational* contact with and use of the inanimate. Regression in analysis to perceptual dedifferentiation of the animate and inanimate realms can be observed and may play an important part in structural change. Empirically, clinicians tend to speak of structural change in the analysand to the extent to which changes have occurred in the quantities and loci of self-experience as originating centers of autonomous action.

Workers in many fields, including the physicist Ilya Prigogine, are today exploring the concept of structure and fundamental differences between animate and inanimate structures. Their work is pertinent to these considerations and will be discussed at length in the final chapter.

In psychoanalytic treatment, issues related to the dedifferentiation of the animate and the inanimate typically surface in connection with specific conflicts in neurotic individuals and are more pervasive in borderline and narcissistic patients. Going somewhat beyond a summary of what I have been discussing in this chapter, *I consider it an important thesis that there is a correspondence between the dichotomies of inner-outer, temporal-spatial, and animate-inanimate (with inner corresponding to temporal and animate, and so on).* Different manifestations of these corresponding dichotomies, however, may dominate the foreground of the clinical landscape of patients with different diagnoses and those at different stages of treatment. The dichotomies occupy a central position in the psychopathology of psychosis, but the dedifferentiation of the animate and the inanimate in severely decompensated and regressed schizophrenic patients is so pervasive and so interwoven with other dedifferentiations (or "fusions") that it is sometimes difficult to demonstrate it specifically.

I would like to conclude this chapter by considering some formal aspects of the countertransference situation, effort and fatigue, and their relationship to diagnostics, therapeutics, and the particular issues I have been discussing here. My basic notion is that diagnostic categories are in some way related to the sense of effort that the therapist or analyst experiences in bringing about change in the patient, specifically change of *conviction*. The relationship between the therapist's sense of effort and the ease of change in the patient is a complex one, however, because the therapist's expectations enter the picture. For instance, an argument could be made that borderline patients are those who initially present themselves in such a way that the therapist *expects* them to act fairly "normally" and to "use insight gained" rather readily, but who subsequently behave more bizarrely and resist change more persistently than expected. In terms of the content of this chapter, they manifest more problems in the area of animate-inanimate differentiation and at the same time threaten the therapist's sense of himself as an effective, animate agent.

Also pertinent here are some observations on my fatigue and on the time of my awareness of different degrees and qualities of fatigue with various kinds of patients. These observations have had some corroboration in the experiences of colleagues. During a period when I was dividing my time between psychoanalytically based therapy with psychotic (mostly schizophrenic) and border-line patients and the psychoanalysis of neurotic patients, I found the day-to-day work more fatiguing with the neurotic patients than with the flagrantly psychotic ones. I found some reversal of this situation, however, upon returning from vacation; often, prior to meeting with a psychotic patient for the first time after a vacation, I was particularly aware of my expectation of hard work. Borderline patients tended to be on both sides of the spectrum—inducing fatigue at most times.

Later I will return to considerations of effort in a broader context, but let me note in anticipation that effort makes no sense if one does not believe that it will produce something worthwhile. Effort is thus tied to the idea of causality. If there is no causal linkage between events, they seem to occur in a haphazard fashion. The idea of the unconscious shrinks the world of the haphazard, since linkages are established or are presumed to exist where previously there seemed to be none. Perceived linkages determine our world, our psychological realities.

At the other extreme from the problem of seeing separate parts and apparent lack of continuity where actually there is unseen continuity is the problem of seeing continuity, a chain of causal connection, where actually there is *none*. An experiment by Bavelas (1970) illustrates this phenomenon. The subject of the experiment is told that there is a correct sequence of punching a group of buttons. A bell will sound, he is told, when he hits upon the correct pattern. The subject's work is rewarded with increasingly frequent bell sounds until the experiment is interrupted. When asked about the correct pattern, the subject describes it and explains which hypotheses he formed, discarded, and modified in the process of becoming totally convinced that he has discovered the right sequence. When the experimenter explains that there is no correct pattern and that the timing of the bell sounds followed a theoretical learning curve, the subject is incredulous. He gives up his conviction only after he hears another subject express a similar certainty in the correctness of a different pattern—that is, when the first subject becomes the experimenter with a second subject who is put through the same set of conditions. The sensation of effort is related to *conviction* and is connected with a representational structure of oneself as an animate center of action. In clinical work, the study of who experiences himself as making what kind of effort, and when, reveals parallels between categories of effort and patients with various degrees and kinds of pathology and sheds some light on the flow of transference and countertransference and trial-identifications.

To return to my main thesis here, when there has been a wrong hookup, so to speak, when a human is experienced as inanimate, a true regression in the analysis occurs and a restructuring not only is essential but may be precipitated by the encounter. The fundamental cannibalistic anxiety of the animate-inanimate boundary—the "raw-cooked" dichotomy—is dealt with in the story of Hansel and Gretel. The witch in the story obviously cannot make the distinction between the animate and the inanimate, and paradoxically it is this nonhuman characteristic that permits Hansel and Gretel to survive. Mistaking stick for finger (unlike the normal human infant), the witch believes the children are not yet fat enough to eat. If we were to psychoanalyze the witch and make it possible for her to integrate the distinction between animate and inanimate on *all* levels of learning, she would not become a more successful witch, but her cannibalistic tendencies would undoubtedly become confined to the ideational or fantasy level. She would be much less prone to *act* like a witch and might deal with cannibalistic fantasies by reading to some children the story of Hansel and Gretel.

Chapter 5

Schizophrenia

The study of schizophrenic patients has played an important part in the formulation of many of the ideas on multiple realities that are central to this book. Once these ideas had been formulated, they were useful in the understanding and treatment of some nonpsychotic disorders as well as schizophrenia. I believe that at a time when the biological study of schizophrenia and the use of pharmacological interventions are in the ascendance, attention to psychodynamic issues of this kind is essential for a balanced approach to the disorder. Organic theories of the etiology of schizophrenia and organic treatments were on the scene long before I started working with such patients, but these early hypotheses and treatments were often disappointing, even damaging (as with frontal lobotomies). I recognize, of course, the contributions of current sophisticated biological research to the understanding and treatment of schizophrenia, and indeed, my own partial model of schizophrenic thought disorder leaves room for a plausible biological contribution. There is, however, the danger that enthusiasm for the new developments and a resultant biological reductionism may lead to the neglect of the important psychosocial observations made by those who have worked with, studied, and managed these patients for years.

For a long time, there has been a tendency among biological

investigators to consider that schizophrenic patients who improved dramatically in the course of psychotherapy with minimal or no pharmacological intervention had been misdiagnosed as schizophrenic or, more simply, had experienced unexplained spontaneous cures. Such "exceptions" should not be ignored. In a yearly lecture, "The Case for the Single Case," Heinrich Klüver used to present the accumulating evidence that the detailed study of the *exception* had led to most major scientific advances. Dynamic and biological study of schizophrenic individuals who are the most pronounced exceptions in a population that statistically shows a correlation between symptomatology and biological findings may help distinguish pathogenic mechanisms from epiphenomena.

Although most experts in schizophrenia these days avoid a primitive polarization between the dynamic and organic approaches, too often they take refuge in a somewhat self-congratulatory claim of favoring a "psychobiosocial" approach. In practice this approach avoids the hard questions of the conceptual, experimental, and therapeutic bridges. In an early investigation that began to tackle such questions, a psychoanalytic study of disorders with a known infectious etiology, paresis, yielded interesting data (Hollos and Ferenczi, 1922). Although the infectious etiology of the disorder was clearly established, and although formal characteristics of the delusional systems of these syphilitic patients had much in common (the familiar themes of delusions of grandeur or persecution), the content of the delusions could best be understood after a detailed, psychoanalytically informed study of the patients' life histories prior to the onset of the organic psychosis.

Another early study, Federn's comparison of anesthesia and normal dreams (1952), examined the influence of pharmacological data on dreaming and led to the understanding of dream modifications resulting from diminished access to mobility. Authors who are currently grappling with the hard conceptual issues include Steven Rose (1980), Karl Pribram (1986), and Morton Reiser (1984), among others. As an example of useful bridging work on an experimental level, one study demonstrated how the experimenter's *words* can influence memory even in individuals whose memory is affected by organic factors (Squire, 1986). I refer specifically to the findings on memory because of the importance I have come to attach to the therapist's efforts to help the schizophrenic patient integrate psychotic and nonpsychotic periods—that is, in some way to remember. In this context the old observation that there is some overlap between certain "organic" and "schizophrenic" diagnostic signs on the Rorschach test also deserves another look.

Finally, therapists who have treated the same patients dynamically prior to and during the period of modern psychopharmacology have a unique longitudinal vantage point. They have noted, for instance, that, in general, brief hospitalizations that emphasize biological treatments seem to be increasing rather than decreasing chronicity. This is only a small example of how essential it is to integrate psychoanalytic and biological modes of thinking about schizophrenia. The collaboration of dynamically (and especially psychoanalytically) trained workers with those who study and treat patients biologically can help navigate research between the shoals of biological oversimplification and psychodynamic rigidity.

Pharmacological studies are often based on large patient populations, but the merits of investigations of individual cases should not be overlooked. Long-term, detailed, intensive study and treatment of single cases permit the filtering out of conceptual and therapeutic fashions and the focusing on ideas that have stood the test of time. Single case studies, therefore, can provide promising hypotheses for formal research strategies. They can also provide some perspective on the integration of the illness into a life history and on the possible effects of therapy on the quality of life, especially during nonpsychotic periods. With these considerations in mind, I will again turn to clinical material, before dealing with more general theoretical issues.

Long-term Psychotherapy in Schizophrenia

Mrs. Dorothy L has been studied and treated psychodynamically both before and during the era of modern psychopharmacology. The emphasis on psychodynamic understanding has not precluded some use of medication, and I will discuss formulations emerging from the interaction of these approaches.

The study of Mrs. L also included two periods of double-blind pharmacological treatment on a schizophrenia research unit. After almost thirty years of work with Mrs. L, I find that certain psycho-analytic concepts and psychoanalytically informed approaches remain pertinent and useful. Some of my dynamic formulations, consistent with but not usually discussed in the analytic framework, have also emerged as important. The patient recently told me that she is thinking of writing a book to be entitled "How to Train One's Therapist." Certain emphases in my presentation are undoubtedly the result of her training activities.

Mrs. L, who is in her late fifties, is the wife of a retired executive and the mother of two children, both of whom are married, have children, and are successful in their professions. Mrs. L's father, Mr. K, was a prominent social science professor, and her mother was a rather eccentric illustrator of children's books. It is likely that Mrs. K had a disturbed period, perhaps a psychotic episode, in her late adolescence or early adult years, during which she was cared for in an attic at home. Mrs. L has a brother two years her junior and an adoptive brother seven years her junior. Both are successful in academic professions.

Dorothy L has often been told that she "tore something" in her mother when she was born. Always a tall, gawky child, she grew into a somewhat awkward adolescent, taller than most of her classmates, including boys. Her mother's lack of interest in the household, particularly anything having to do with food preparation, was striking. Meals consisted of little more than bread and water when there was no maid to prepare them. Mr. K's protectiveness of his wife went very far, and once when one of Dorothy's brothers started to complain about a particularly inadequate meal, Mr. K silently picked him up and carried him out of the room. Early pictures of Dorothy generally show a depressed expression and neglected grooming. Throughout her childhood and into adolescence, however, an aunt and a grandfather regularly took Dorothy away from her parental home, especially during the long summer months. As the only child in the alternative home, she was pampered, sometimes dressed up a bit like a doll, but always the subject of much genuine attention and affection; the household staff, which included cook, maid, and chauffeur, acquiesced to all her requests and treated her like a little princess. (There are indications that different ego-states during the course of her treatment are related to her two homes.)

Socially quite isolated in school, bossy with the brother closer in age, protective and affectionate with her younger brother, she became a hardworking and excellent student. She was consistently a teacher's pet, and her teacher's expressions of approval are important memories sustaining her at times of shattered self-esteem. Some pictures show Dorothy as an adolescent imitating elements of her father's clothing. She describes some outings with her father during which she experienced what can only be called fulfillment. She came very close to experiencing herself as his only son and sometimes also as his caretaking wife.

Dorothy had started attending college away from home during World War II but soon obeyed a call to return to the then maternal household because Mr. K had an important assignment overseas. Dorothy felt that she was summoned home to counterbalance her mother's erratic behavior, perhaps to cook for her younger siblings whenever the maid was not available. The summons home also interrupted an important romantic relationship with a fellow student. While at home, Dorothy was quite depressed; the level of her performance in some part-time courses dropped markedly, and she attempted to combat her marked isolation through brief contacts with young soldiers. She then enlisted in the women's corps of one of the armed services.

After a few months there, at the age of twenty-one, she experienced her first diagnosed schizophrenic episode. Her peers and superiors had noticed her withdrawal, neglect of her body and clothing, marked deterioration of her functioning and work, probably some delusions and paranoid ideation, and some grotesque overconscientiousness. She precipitated her hospitalization by swallowing, in front of an officer, a medication intended for external treatment of a minor skin disorder. She was hospitalized briefly and then given a medical discharge from the service. During the next ten years, prior to my contact with her, she functioned sometimes marginally, sometimes well. She married and bore two children. She also had some psychotic episodes. Treatment modalities included psychotherapy, insulin, and electroconvulsive shock.

I have seen Dorothy L in almost continuous psychotherapy, ranging in frequency from five hours to one hour per week, for the past thirty years. During her lifetime she has been hospitalized fifteen times for a total of about nine years. No regularity or rhythmicity has been noted in the psychiatric hospitalizations. The longest period of continuous hospitalization, in the early 1960s, was four years; the shortest, one week. The total time spent in halfway houses, day hospitals, and similar arrangements is four years. She has demonstrated a wide range of schizophrenic symptomatology, including systematized paranoid features and such catatonic features as waxy flexibility, mutism, refusal to eat, and retention of urine and feces of such severity that the consulting internist feared permanent bowel damage. It must be emphasized, however, that during nonpsychotic periods the level of her intellectual and social functioning has frequently been very high. She was actively involved in the raising of her children, had a moderately busy social life, traveled abroad, studied languages and music, and was an appreciated volunteer in groups supporting artistic endeavors.

The varying lengths of hospitalization are related in part to changes in the evolving philosophy of treatment. Although I was greatly influenced by the work of Paul Federn, one of the first psychoanalysts to treat schizophrenic patients (perhaps *the* first), my approach differed significantly from his from the beginning in one respect. Federn had suggested that when in remission the patient should be treated by a therapist other than the one working with him or her during the acute phases of schizophrenia. For a variety of reasons, I wanted to explore the possibilities of bridge building between these phases by having the patient during nonpsychotic phases deal with the content brought to the surface during acute psychotic phases. This treatment approach was thought to be safer in a hospital setting, and the longest period of hospitalization was intended to serve this purpose. I have continued with the bridge-building approach, since the patient gradually became more accepting of hospitalization when it was needed. It became possible to treat her more intensively on an outpatient basis and to hospitalize her only when necessary.

Mrs. L's early admissions to hospitals could be very dramatic.

She was agitated and belligerent, arrived at the hospital in an ambulance with sirens blowing, and needed to be restrained by several strong attendants. Typical of more recent hospitalizations was her hallucinating my office in her vacation home at the beginning of decompensation. At that point, she obeyed my hallucinated suggestion to check into a hospital.

Clinical observations supported by double-blind studies of Mrs. L indicate that remissions occur without the use of medication, and that remissions that perhaps occurred more quickly because of pharmacologic intervention were maintained for long periods when medication was stopped. So far, prolonged periods of medication with this patient do not seem to have been effective prophylactically. Although this does not rule out the possibility of finding a prophylactically effective medication regime, to date a limited use of medication at specific times, determined by symptomatic fluctuations and variations in her response to psychotherapeutic intervention, seems to offer more advantages in her treatment. The following medications have been used: perphenazine, amitriptyline, chlorpromazine, trifluoperazine, thioridazine, prolixin, fluphenazine, and lithium carbonate.

Some biological data will complete the background material on Dorothy L. Two brain ventricular measurements of 8.4 percent are probably within the normal range for her age group. The prostaglandin E_1 (PGE1)—stimulated cyclic AMP production in the platelets of this patient—is abnormally low. Dr. M. Kafka has pointed out that this abnormality found in schizophrenic patients could conceivably be only in platelets, but is probably in the neuron as well. As the cyclic AMP probably mediates phosphorylation and activation of cellular proteins in neurons as well as platelets, a decrease in the cyclic AMP concentration intracellularly could modulate the rate and magnitude of transmission in the brain. If transmission is altered, perhaps it plays a role in the pathophysiology of schizophrenia (M. S. Kafka et al., 1980).

Although the concepts formulated about Mrs. L's condition and the therapeutic techniques used are intertwined, I will first outline the range of therapeutic techniques:

1. Carefully timed introduction of psychotic material during nonpsychotic periods.

2. Use of cold wet-sheet packs during catatonic episodes at times when she was *not* agitated. (Crude rationale: Outer control should diminish need for inner control.) Verbal therapy was used when the patient was in the sheet pack.

3. During nonpsychotic periods, use of a verbal therapy that at times could be described as close to classical psychoanalysis if this particular segment of treatment were seen outside the context of her overall treatment.

4. Increasing use of interpretive, psychoanalytically based therapy during periods of transition between psychotic and nonpsychotic states. It is here that the combination of pharmacotherapy and psychotherapy can be particularly important because the transition phases may be shortened and the patient can be confronted with material she produced very recently.

The following clinical notes are from one of my therapeutic hours with the patient. They illustrate the kind of psychoanalytically based therapy that can be done with schizophrenics during phases that are transitional between overtly psychotic and nonpsychotic states.

The patient experiences a big bowel movement as loss of her inner organs. She describes confusion between anal and vaginal orifices, feels that some skin is missing, and says she feels "something has been cut off." Direct interpretation of castration fear is made and related to her previously experienced delusional identification with men, particularly her father. I remind her of a photograph of herself in which she is wearing a tie and other male clothing.

The patient asks me to hospitalize her. She tells me that previously she has denied that she is crazy, but now she knows she is. She demonstrates this by a delusional preoccupation with dirt, which characterized many of her hospitalized periods. She has to wash every few minutes; she says the insulin with which she was treated many years ago is coming out of her hair and then tells me she has relapsed because she has masturbated. It is possible for her to accept the idea that her preoccupation with dirt is connected with masturbation. She makes clear to me that her view of the functioning society lady is incompatible with her view of herself as someone who on rare occasions masturbates. She is visibly relieved when I tell her that sometimes she asks for hospitalization because she cannot live up to the idealized society role at all times. She is incredulous when I suggest that she go to one of her volunteer functions despite the fact that she has masturbated. She asks about the "after-effects" of masturbation.

She describes a tightness in her lower abdomen which keeps her from sleeping. It becomes clear that the tightness being discussed now, when she is an outpatient, is related to the retention of feces during her previous hospitalization. It is an attempt to hold on tightly, to prevent the loss of an imaginary penis. She interprets sexual flush as a punishing change in her body. As in other sessions, we discuss bodily sensations in minute detail, and her interpretations of them. Her guilt feelings related to her having "torn something" in her mother are part of the picture.

At times it has been useful to classify and describe to Mrs. L resistances that manifest themselves in (1) her not recognizing connections (for example, masturbation and general dirt preoccupation) and (2) her insisting on false connections (for example, punishment and sexual flush).

Therapeutic work of this kind has led me to the following conceptual formulations:

1. Reexamination of the very concept of schizophrenic thought disorder: The *constant objects* (often more "abstract," more "atmospheric," less related to individual persons) are different from those of nonschizophrenic patients. The thought operations *on* these objects are not.[1]

2. Reformulation of double-bind theory: Parental intolerance of ambiguity rather than paradoxical communication is seen as a pathogenic factor (as elaborated in chapter 2).

3. A refinement of the concept of the therapeutic window: The patient is seen as going in and out of psychotic states very rapidly, making microchanges within seconds, too rapidly for a therapeutic window in the usual sense. (This formulation is related to the notion of the recapitulation of the ontogeny of perception.) Therefore, the therapist who communicates on different levels of complexity at the same time is more likely to be heard by the patient.

---

1. Ordinary logic is used in thinking and talking about those idiosyncratic objects. "Heidi-ness," for instance, has an identity. To illustrate the point schematically, it is conceivable that the therapist would ask the patient: "Please introduce me to Heidi-ness." This would be more congruent with the patient's object world than if he were to ask her to introduce him to Heidi (see chapter 2).

4. An interpretation of the patient's understanding of psychotic symptoms: As the patient decompensates and moves toward the psychotic state, the *last organization* available is *oral* and often is clearly oral rage. I have come to understand that the patient interprets the diminution of her functioning as punishment for something she has done or failed to do. Since primitive oral aggression is in the foreground, the punishment itself is perceived as oral aggression directed toward her. My dealing with the psychotic material she produces is perceived by her as an attack coming from me, an attack full of oral rage. My interpretation of her understanding of her own psychotic symptoms as punishment sometimes interrupts the vicious cycle.

In the last formulation, the central point is the patient's aversion to dealing with psychotic material, even when there is no outright denial. It is this aversion, I believe, that led Federn to recommend a different therapist during the nonpsychotic states. When the same therapist remains in the picture, however, the interpretation linking psychosis itself with attack ("It is as if I were biting you when I don't let you off the hook and tell you that we just can't ignore these crazy things if you want the benefits of not always living in a crazy world") helps establish the therapist in both worlds. When this occurs at times of the patient's transition between psychotic and nonpsychotic organizations, the link between content (biting, for instance) and the formal characteristics of psychotic organization or disorganization can be of use in establishing some continuity. At such periods of transition, incidentally, because of the complex mechanisms of projection and projective identification and the looseness of ego boundaries, biting or other forms of violent aggression are in the "atmosphere," and it matters little whether analyst or patient is referred to as the "biter."

If one has had the experience of working intensively for a long time and in many different ways with schizophrenic patients, some recent descriptions of psychotherapeutic approaches seem peculiarly fragmented. I do not want to minimize the relative effectiveness of such approaches, which include "supportive" and other "intensive forms of individual psychotherapy" and "psychoeducational" and other forms of family therapy (see, for instance,

Gunderson and Carroll, 1983; Anderson, 1983). But it is important not to lose sight of the usefulness of the whole range of approaches that psychotherapists have employed with schizophrenic patients.

Miss R, for example, had been hospitalized in several institutions for over twenty years when I started working with her. Despite massive electroconvulsive treatment, she had remained intermittently and unpredictably violent, so that she had spent the greater part of many years in isolation rooms. I will not describe my work with this patient, which lasted well over a decade, in detail here, but I will highlight the range of techniques I used in order to provide some contrast with what I consider more "fractionated" approaches.

After prolonged observation, I arrived at the opinion that Miss R had several different psychotic organizations. I coined for myself the term *multiple psychotic personalities*, which incorporates the recognition of such varying dissociations. At times she was receptive to my calling attention to such differences in her mental organization and in her functioning. Therapeutic work around this issue led to her asking for cold wet-sheet packs when she sensed the possible eruption of violence. This development permitted a whole socializing approach. I taught her to use the telephone and to eat in restaurants, and I brought her to my home. I also met her family, making it clear that I was *not* the family's therapist and that I would feel free to tell her what I learned from the family but not vice versa. The meetings with the family, with or without her present, were only occasional and, of course, were in addition to the four or five weekly individual sessions with Miss R. I also went with her, her social worker, and several aides to the family's home and had meetings with all of them in this setting.

Since my purpose here is to describe the range of activities, I will not give in detail characteristics of the family structure, but will mention only a family secret that came to light—namely, the suspicion that in a previous generation, when an attempt to arrange a shot-gun wedding of an unmarried pregnant family member had failed, the reluctant groom was killed. This story, or perhaps myth, hung like a cloud over this conservative, religious, and puritanical family. If some topics have to be avoided at all costs—topics that could in some way lead to, be reminiscent of, or be associated with the theme of a secret (or myth)—the range of permitted topics can become remarkably narrow. In this case, anything having to do with sex, pregnancy, grooming, looks, fun, dancing, youth, and similar subjects was strictly taboo. Religion, with an emphasis on religious fears, was a pervasive but not much talked-about presence in the family. The permitted verbal topics did not extend much beyond work, business, and financial matters in this wealthy family. Miss R apparently referred to this focus, the specialized financial vocabulary, but also to the narrow range of topics that could be put into words when she called the family's way of speaking their "gangster language." My experiences with Miss R contributed to my expectation that etiologically oriented family studies will continue to be important in the study of the determinants of schizophrenic pathology. I look forward to the results of such studies as those of Helgard Roeder, at the Max Planck Institute in Munich, who is rigorously testing earlier family hypotheses formulated by Lidz and others, using computer-based technology (see Lidz and Fleck, 1960; Stierlin et al., 1983; in the latter volume, see particularly contributions by Wynne and the Finnish Adoptive Family Studies by Tienari et al.).

Miss R's references to "wide" and "narrow" language contributed to the development of my ideas about schizophrenic objects. These objects are atmospheric. It gradually became clear that Miss R's wide language was poetic and referred to an emotional atmosphere; sometimes it reflected only internal states expressed metaphysically, but often it included amalgamated references to external conditions and internal states. "There was an earthquake last night" referred to the patient's emotional agitation, but also to general unrest on the ward during the preceding night. Utilitarian language—ordering food in a restaurant or instructing a telephone operator—was narrow language, and so was her family's "gangster" language. Miss R's *calling* it "gangster" language is, however, an example of wide language. Her reaction to family members' preoccupations, her own reaction to what they do in the financial world, reference to the possible murder in the family secret or myth and the associated caution, the restriction of permissible topics—all are part of the "gangster" atmosphere. It was this patient whom I observed walking faster than usual when she said the earth was shrinking. I thought of Miss R and other schizophrenic patients when I read in "The Innerworld of the Outerworld of the Innerworld" (Handke, 1969, p. 128):

> We find ourselves in a department store:
> we want to use the escalator
> to get to the toy department
> where we want to purchase building blocks
> but since the escalator has temporarily stopped
> the immobile escalator
> on which we were walking up
> transforms itself into our breath
> which we are holding
> and the held breath
> which we now exhale
> because the escalator is suddenly moving again
> implodes into a pile of building blocks—

Wide language for Miss R also seemed to be the language of contemplation and had a temporal meaning—contrasted with efficient, quick, and focused communication. She agreed to use such narrow language only after repeated reassurances that she could return to the wide one and after I had demonstrated many times that I could switch back and forth in my own use of the two forms of communication. Usually Miss R's physical movements were slow, even, and remarkably deliberate. For years, however, there had been occasional short periods of agitation and physical aggression which gradually diminished and eventually disappeared during my years of work with her. I have sometimes considered whether her fear of being permanently shackled into a narrow world of communication and experience had contributed to her agitation. Her learning that she did not have to abandon one world to live in another may have played a part in the fading of the occasional furious agitation.[2]

2. When I discuss Miss R's possible revolt against narrowness, I should also mention the circumscribed role that had been envisaged for her since early childhood. Somehow she was the one who was expected not to get married and to become the parents' caretaker in their old age. These specific limited expectations could have contributed to the subsequent apparently bizarre disregard of her own needs and individuality. Two years older than her sister, she was kept from going to school until both sisters, dressed alike, could be driven to school together.

Usually Miss R was far from agitated. She was unsurpassed in her skill with the most complicated jigsaw puzzles. She would sit quietly in front of the puzzle pieces, hardly moving for as long as ten or sometimes twenty minutes, and then slowly place a piece, deliberately and precisely. Even placements made early in her work on the puzzle never needed subsequent revision or correction. The deliberation shown in this task also characterized the way in which she ordinarily seemed to survey both the external world and her internal state. The wide language, as I have noted, reflected both. It was in the context of my psychoanalytically based therapeutic efforts that I came to understand something of her narrow and wide languages and of her fear that she would lose one if she used the other. This in turn permitted me to teach her to use narrow language when I went with her to restaurants and when she once again began to use the telephone. Dynamic approaches do not preclude such instructional and behavioral techniques. They give them dignity and meaning and, I believe, enhance their effectiveness. Still, it would not be difficult to find in Miss R's wide language remaining evidence of schizophrenic thought disorder. She has, however, learned the difference between wide and narrow worlds—and has apparently learned techniques for protecting them both well enough to have lived for many years now—without medication—outside the hospital.

Assessing the Dreams of Schizophrenics

Although I have not thus far dealt explicitly with the "separate reality" of dreams, I hypothesize that incomplete recapitulation of the ontogeny of perception plays a part in differentiating dream objects from objects of normal working life. In dreams, as in psychosis, some perceptual processes are carried further than others. This produces the "idiosyncrasies" of dream objects. The differences between dreams and psychotic phenomena certainly deserve further study, but for now I remain in the company of those who emphasize their similarities.

If schizophrenic conditions have much in common with dreams, what thoughts and clinical data can we organize around the theme of dreams in schizophrenia? So many questions about

SCHIZOPHRENIA

schizophrenia and its treatment remain unanswered that I consider
dealing with the clinical use of dreams with patients in this condition something of a tour de force, but some thoughts have crystal-
lized for me. I do not *generally* consider the clinical use of dreams
of central importance in therapeutic work with schizophrenic patients, but at times it may be. There are also interesting similarities
and differences in ways of using dream material in the treatment of
these and other patients. In a two-part article, Grotstein (1977) has
elaborated such material in relation to the etiology of schizophrenia. In my own day-to-day therapeutic work, however, I have
depended more on some relatively simple ideas—such as the use
of dreams in the "bridging" therapeutic approach, the "evacuation" function of dreams, trauma in the life and dreams of schizophrenics, the repair of psychosis through dreams, and several
other related themes. I shall briefly elaborate these various ways of
making use of the dreams of schizophrenics.

It is in connection with the bridging approach in the work with
schizophrenic patients that dreams have their most explicit application. Some relapses of schizophrenic patients into acute psychosis are not yet well understood, whether we try to understand
them biologically, psychodynamically, or through combined approaches. Earlier in my career, I would have announced some
"understandings" that I do not now claim. Over the years too
many different "understandings" have been required for the same
kind of relapse in the same patient. I believe, however, that the
bridging therapeutic approach I mentioned earlier—having one
therapist stay with the patient in times of relapse—has helped to
avert further relapses in some patients, to diminish their frequency
and duration in other patients, and certainly to lessen the impact of
recurrences on the lives of patients and family members.

The topic of the continuity of the content of the psychosis in
dream material has been developed by Douglas Noble (1951) and
by Clarence G. Schulz (Schulz and Kilgalen, 1969). The latter two
wrote about work with a severely disturbed schizophrenic patient
who began to relate dreams after about five months of psychotherapy: "As his behavior began to improve, his psychotic thinking decreased and he began to report dreams" (p. 20). The dreams

mirrored the antecedent psychotic material. It is possible that this sequence—from psychotic material to dream—is particularly clear in patients with a history of readily identifiable trauma. One aspect of the history of Schulz's patient was that his two siblings had died under tragic circumstances in separate accidents. I will return shortly to the use of dreams in the psychotherapy of schizophrenic patients with a fairly obvious traumatic history of this kind.

Another idea in the literature that has evoked an echo in my own clinical experience concerns the function of "evacuation." With reservations that will be spelled out gradually, I have found what André Green says about work with borderline patients to be applicable at times in work with schizophrenic patients:

> Dream analysis . . . is, as a rule, unproductive. . . . Dreams do not express wish-fulfillment but rather serve a function of evacuation. . . . The dream barrier is an important function of the psychic apparatus. . . . Even though the dream barrier is effective, the dream's purpose is not the working through of instinct derivatives, but rather the unburdening of the psychic apparatus from painful stimuli. . . . The dreams . . . are not characterized by condensation but by concretization. One can also observe dream failures in these patients: wakening in order to prevent dreaming or to find themselves surrounded by a strange, disquieting atmosphere, which constitutes a transitional dream state akin to a nightmare. In more successful instances, dreams are actualizations of the self in the dream space, attempts to reformulate traumatic experiences. . . . In such instances, the most significant thing in analyzing a dream is not the dream's latent content but *the dreamer's experience*. (1977, p. 38)

Whatever our eventual understanding of the etiology of various schizophrenic disorders, for immediate therapeutic and practical working purposes, I find that I function as though I believed that trauma was etiologically more important for some schizophrenic patients than for others. I think, for instance, of Eleanor M, who had her first acute episode after she had acquiesced to her mother's request that she be present in the operating room during the mother's exploratory surgery; when the mother was opened up, she was found to have a widespread malignancy. Eleanor was also the main caretaker of her dying mother, and the notion that a sedative she gave her mother killed her was at times an important element in her delusions.

Eleanor was diagnosed as schizophrenic on the basis of all the usual criteria by the staffs of several hospitals. She showed particularly flamboyant pathology; hallucinating and wildly agitated, she was denudative, smeared herself and the walls of seclusion rooms with menstrual blood, and was destructive of property and sometimes assaultive. During more than fifteen years of psychotherapeutic work with her, I found the role of dreams in her treatment an important one, as I shall describe below.

Eleanor was eventually able to leave the hospital, the frequency and severity of acute episodes diminished radically, and during the last eight years only one brief hospitalization was necessary. (Medication, on the whole, did not play a significant role in her management or treatment.) When she did not need to be hospitalized, Eleanor functioned quite well as a wife, mother, and participating member in community affairs. Her preoccupation with violence in her waking life was limited to a fascination with crime and criminals, wars, and catastrophes. Her selection of movies, television shows, and newspaper and magazine articles was almost exclusively based on such interests. Her dream life was characterized by prolonged periods during which she reported hundreds of rather repetitive dreams dealing with amputations, mutilations, and bloody scenes.

Thus, Eleanor presented contrasting pictures: she was prim and proper when not psychotic, but her dream life and psychotic periods were full of gore. Over the years of working with her, I developed a technique of using gory language in talking about her dreams and impulses ("You wanted to smash her skull and smear her brains all over the wall"). But again and again I told her my reasons for doing so, spelling out the idea that her attempts to compartmentalize such material might contribute to the psychotic episodes. In Eleanor's treatment there were long periods when the therapy resembled some of the therapeutic work done with cases of battle fatigue during and after World War II. (For example, war movies were shown to soldiers who had experienced major dissociative episodes in battle. Showings of these movies were interrupted from time to time, and when the lights went on, Red Cross girls offered the soldiers tea.)

Despite the use of such techniques, recognition of transference elements and the genetics of the conflict had their place in Eleanor's treatment. The emphasis was, however, as André Green put it, "not [on] the dream's latent content but the dreamer's experience."

From the literature on dreams in schizophrenia and psychosis, I will cite one further notion that is in harmony with my own clinical use of dreams with these patients. In a 1953 paper, Eissler refers to a psychotic patient who in her dreams repairs the psychosis, so to speak. It is as if the dreaming ego were nonpsychotic while the waking ego was psychotic. Eissler notes that similar observations were made by Freud and mentions Freud's notion that "reality" appears like an instinct derivative in dreams of psychotics. That is, it was Freud's belief that the psychotic individual had constructed for himself a world that was so different and distinct from reality—I would say from commonsense reality—that ordinary reality broke through into dreams in the same way in which material related to "instinct" broke into dreams of the nonpsychotic individual. Although oversimplified, these references to Eissler's and Freud's notions are related to the following clinical observations.

I accidentally discovered many years ago that when I awakened Andrew, a hospitalized schizophrenic patient with a complex paranoid delusional system, he was apparently free of delusions for five or ten minutes. I could never obtain from the patient any confirmation that he was dreaming, and any possible "repair" of the psychosis could have been the work of merely the "sleeping ego" and not necessarily of the "dreaming ego." In any case, the psychosis seemed to have been temporarily repaired during his sleep, when psychoticlike dream material occurs in the nonpsychotic individual. This repair of the psychosis was always carried over into the waking state for seven minutes (as I worked with this patient, I found it interesting to time it precisely), after which the delusions were reestablished.

Another patient, John M, had been diagnosed as schizophrenic during several prolonged hospitalizations and at one time prior to

my acquaintance with him had received a series of electroconvulsive treatments. His symptoms were such that some clinicians
would consider him as having a severe borderline disorder with
pronounced narcissistic features. He did have frankly psychotic
periods during my years of work with him, and brief hospitalizations were required, although drug abuse made it difficult to identify the precipitating factors. Dreams were important in my work
with John, but my treatment of him was more consistently psychoanalytic, and my clinical use of dreams did not differ significantly
from psychoanalytic dream interpretations. One feature of his
dream reports, however, may relate to Eissler's observation. He
often said very emphatically that his dreams now contained some
"distortions." A room in which he lived or a landscape that he
remembered from his childhood differed from the way it "really"
was. Ordinarily, nonpsychotic dreamers consider such distortions
to be part of the usual fabric of the dream. For John they were
"unusual" in comparison with what he considered his *normal*
dreams. During psychotic episodes, he had apparently experienced dreams in which there was much "undistorted" reality.
Clinically he was able to use my observations relating to such
fluctuations in his dreams in a bridging fashion. My observations
served as an introduction to part of normal living—namely, normally distorted dreams. Furthermore, I learned to use the degree of
distortion he reported about his dream material as an indicator of
his distance from a psychotic episode, and such observations
helped in his management.

As an elaborated example of this kind of reversal, one month
after a psychiatric hospitalization, Dorothy L reported dreaming
that her mother was dead, her father was alive, and another woman
was embracing him. The patient's actual life situation at that time
was that her *father* was dead and her *mother* was living. She
emphasized that the scene reminded her of some Picasso paintings
of his Blue Period, and further commented, "It's an interesting
dream; the female figure is of undetermined age." Her sexual
interest in her father had been an explicitly recognized theme in my
prolonged work with her. During acute psychotic episodes she also
was fused with, transformed into, or partially blended with her

father. At one time, for instance, she made a point of not shaving her legs because "I have father's legs."

In addition to the patient's emphases on Picasso's Blue Period, some of her other associations involved her daughter (who liked Picasso), a period in her daughter's life when she was developing breasts, a visit to a relative who was divorcing her husband, and the patient's wish that her father had divorced her mother. In many respects these dream elements were understood by Dorothy L and were interpreted much as a neurotic patient might comprehend her own dream material after prolonged insight-oriented therapy or analysis. She explained, however, that she could have such a dream now "because last month has been going very well. My husband did not go on any trips. He cooked a lot of dinners." She then talked about her father's flirtations but discussed love very explicitly in terms of who fed whom. Mother did not feed father well; therefore, she did not love him. She made precise equations in energy terms. She could have this dream now because she had been well fed during the previous month and consequently had enough energy to work on the old problems of her father's death.

In my experience, when a schizophrenic patient can talk about the *dreamlike* atmosphere of a dream, and does not see everyday reality as the intruder in the dream, then the patient is most removed from a psychotic ego organization. In prolonged psycho-therapeutic work with a schizophrenic patient such a period should not be ignored. The therapist can at such a moment deal explicitly with the apparently "neurotic" conflicts that are being presented and dealt with in the dream, but the therapist can also at such a moment introduce a discussion of the changes such material under-goes during psychotic episodes. With Dorothy L, for example, the topic of her wish to be close to her father, to be with her father, could be introduced in an effort to form a bridge between the current and the psychotic states. In the long run such an approach permits the patient to use the image of the therapist in the bridging management of her own psychosis.

On the other hand, I have also encountered in a nonpsychotic patient, Robert S, specific fear of a psychotic reaction when the vividness of the dreams was extreme—for instance, when in his dream he not only saw his own face as that of an animal but also touched his face and discovered that his skin possessed the texture of an animal's skin. Although Robert never actually was psychotic, several family members had been hospitalized with a diagnosis of schizophrenia, and his fear of psychosis was never far from the surface.

Michael, another patient—about whose schizophrenic diagnosis there was no doubt but who lived most of his life outside a hospital—made all kinds of commitments, pledged charitable contributions, and accepted invitations when he actually answered the telephone but then believed that he had dreamt the whole thing. By the time I started working with him, he had already developed a method to circumvent this problem. Since Michael did not know if he was awake or dreaming (he had multiple dreams within dreams) and since pinching himself didn't do the trick, he had learned always to ask, "What is your number? I'll call you back."

Some of the above observations tend to move away from the clinical use of dreams in the therapy of schizophrenic patients. They are nevertheless pertinent. For some patients there seem to be common elements in dreams and psychotic experience—at the very least, there are fears that certain dream characteristics herald psychotic experiences. In working therapeutically for prolonged periods with such patients, the therapist is likely to discover characteristics of dream reports that are indexes of the closeness to the surface of some psychotic phenomena. An index may be valid for only one particular patient because it depends not only on general characteristics of schizophrenic and dream processes but also on such personality variables as intelligence and intellectual style and on various characteristics of patient and therapist that determine the nature of their relationship and communication.

If one works long enough, even with deeply regressed, chronic, or deteriorated patients, one often discovers periods of relatively greater accessibility during which both content and formal elements of dream experiences can be considered collaboratively with the patient. Despite my overall recognition of the general uselessness of too much "intellect" in therapeutic endeavors, I have become less afraid of an "intellectual" approach with some patients at such junctures. It connotes a respect for formal characteristics of the patient's thought—a respect that has a therapeutic function in itself. If one has traveled with a patient for a long time, in and out of psychosis, the intellectual approach has a different cast. The interpretation of the psychosis as an attack is a case in point. Recall Dorothy L, who sought voluntary hospitalization after she hallucinated my instructing her to do so when she was disturbed. Discussion of the form and content of dream material with the patient had been one of the tools useful in facilitating such a development—that is, previous discussion with Dorothy of the form and content of dreams enhanced her ability to observe critically some of her psychotic experiences, even with the therapist only psychologically present.

The primary-process concept is essential for an understanding of the similarities in the formation of dreams and of psychotic thought content. It can clarify for the therapist such practical problems as, for example, the equivalences and fusions of various family members in the mind of the waking schizophrenic patient (Kafka and McDonald, 1965).

Certain characteristics of the dreams of schizophrenic patients can also give the therapist information about the patient's control techniques or methods of self-management. Robert S—the patient with the telephone-answering difficulties—often had "geological" dreams. Geology was one of his daytime interests, and the immensely long and slow time scale of geological events was a clue to his self-management style. One day I told him that I was reminded of a riddle popular in the Swiss city of Bern, whose inhabitants have a reputation for slowness. One Bern citizen asks another, "What is this?" while very slowly drawing an angular line in the air. The correct answer is "lightning." Very, very slowly the patient dared to break—or should I say melt—into a smile. After this it was possible for me to comment on certain catastrophic geological events in his dreams and to relate them in a therapeutically meaningful way to events in his life.

Rather than discuss the nature of the obsessive elements in the defensive structure of Robert S, I will focus on the relative *completeness* of his slow-motion perception and self-perception, and the relative completeness and appropriateness of his gradually developing affective responses. His perceptual acts recapitulated the development of perception rather slowly; he could understand the slow "flash." For this patient such qualities as "suspendedness" could have a defensively useful "quasi object constancy."

Considerations of this kind have a possible connection to the question of concreteness or "concretization" versus abstract qualities in the dreams of schizophrenic patients—and perhaps also in schizophrenic thinking generally. In chapter 3, writing about "abstract expressionism" in dreams, I gave an example of a dream consisting of a continuous line with small wiggles in it. To the dreamer, a therapist reporting a dream after an LSD experience, the line clearly represented the course of history, and the wiggle represented the Holocaust. I have come to believe that this kind of dream experience corresponds in large measure to the waking experience of many schizophrenic patients, for whom certain abstractions carry a bewildering but convincing richness of meaning or meanings. As I indicated earlier, I have been impressed by the contrasting concreteness and vividness—"the reality"—of some "schizophrenic" dreams (always remembering that in the most acute phases, dreams are not reported, and the question is thus irrelevant for therapeutic purposes). If abstract expressionist elements in waking experience have been recognized by the therapist, this may facilitate the patient's reporting the reversal in dream characteristics that, as I pointed out earlier, sometimes occurs at stages of considerable improvement—that is, a dream "atmosphere" becomes more common in dreams along with more "concreteness" in daily living.

In sum, despite our uncertainties in understanding schizophrenic phenomena and despite the observation that the most clearly schizophrenic patients—*when* they are most clearly schizophrenic—do not report dream material, it is apparent that dreams can be used in the treatment of schizophrenia. Recently, as a psychoanalytic consultant to a schizophrenia research unit studying various vigorous pharmacological interventions, I noted that in some patients whose condition changed and fluctuated rapidly, the reporting of dreams could occur almost immediately after emergence from the most severe disorganization. Dream material might be reported when delusions were still very active. The overlapping of acute psychotic manifestations and the reporting of dreams were greater here than I had observed in situations where no such forceful pharmacological interventions were attempted. I would, therefore, anticipate that the study and perhaps the therapeutic use of dreams in schizophrenia may become of greater interest to clinicians with a variety of theoretical orientations.

A Multiple-Reality Approach to Schizophrenic Disorders

Clinicians trying to work with schizophrenic patients face difficulties because simultaneously they know so little about schizophrenia and yet seem to know so much. Inasmuch as therapists may be dealing with a disease of meaning, schizophrenia presents itself as an ideal projective test, a picture into which they can read meaning—and we clinicians can read much that is personal to us into schizophrenic phenomenology. Because we cannot long survive, much less operate, in a vacuum of cause and effect, we constantly try to see and respond to meaning. The longer I have worked with schizophrenic patients, the more I have tended not to discount these projective potentials. To summarize, my ideas have been organized around the following points: (1) during schizophrenic episodes, the patient's important objects become idiosyncratic, specifiably different from those established during ordinary object-constancy formation; (2) the study of the ontogeny of perception offers clues concerning the formation of these idiosyncratic objects; and (3) the resulting theoretical formulations lead to therapeutic strategies based on the effort to comprehend idiosyncratic objects, to confront the patient with a multichannel approach to possible meaning and affect, and, especially, to help the patient to experience the therapist as a constant object in the patient's fluctuating object world.

Simple notions underlie every clinical experiment, and that is what therapeutic work with schizophrenic patients is today. As I indicated in describing the treatment of Dorothy L, one of my clinical experiments has been the use of cold wet-sheet packs in an unorthodox way. These are customarily used to restrain very agitated patients, but I have used them for catatonic patients who were immobile and mute. The crude formulation on which this therapeutic maneuver was based was the hypothesis that the patients were afraid that any movement would destroy the world. Perhaps if I kept them from moving, they would be able to tell me something. When such patients were kept in packs, some of them did begin to speak. But is this confirmation of the hypothesis concerning world-destruction fantasies, and is it solid confirmation that the pack's effectiveness resides in the substitution of external for internal controls?

One belief that has taken on significance for me in terms of my experience is that the very effort to see meaning can have some therapeutic effect. Although this belief, too, should be subjected to verification, some of my therapeutic strategies are based on it. For example, if a schizophrenic patient is wildly gesticulating and obviously hallucinating, it is important for me to enter the scene somehow. In one such instance, because of previous work with Peter, whom I mentioned briefly in chapter 3, I thought the hallucinations had something to do with his father. When I asked some questions about his hallucinations, the patient said, "Louder," and continued saying that until I finally shouted. At this point the patient said, with an expression of disgust, "Not you." I had succeeded in making my presence felt; he had noticed me, despite the hallucinations. Somewhat later in the session, he did respond to some of my questions. If I really wanted to know whether he was hallucinating father or God, he could give me an answer: either father or God would be correct. Although he felt it was a stupid question, he conveyed to me that someone or something in authority was communicating to him. He knew that people make a distinction between father and God, but it was not pertinent. His gesturing (he pointed to something high in the room) indicated that some high authority was communicating with him. This seemed both very abstract and very concrete to me, but I too had entered the scene. I had become a presence; my voice interfered somewhat with the authoritative voice to which he listened. Although he derogated me, I deserved an explanation.

My idea that some of the schizophrenic's objects can be "characteristics" rather than individuals, and therefore quite different from commonsense objects or the usual psychoanalytic ones, led to the notion of the "latent family" of the schizophrenic patient behind the manifest family (Kafka and McDonald, 1965). One patient conveyed that all the blue-eyed members of her family were interchangeable; in effect, they were the same—one object. In her mid-thirties, the patient had rather suddenly had a flagrant schizophrenic episode. But one day when I was walking with the patient and her husband on the hospital grounds I caught a glimpse of a different onset of the illness. With a fixed, laughing expression, the patient looked at her husband and said, "You're not my blue-eyed husband." He laughingly responded, "No, I'm not." When I asked him if she had been saying things like that for a long time, he responded, "Oh, yes. She's been joking like that since before we were married." So much for the acute psychotic episode! The techniques for obscuring psychotic phenomenology in some families (that is, the ability of some families to absorb psychosis) are remarkable.

In chapter 2, when discussing Arieti's quotation of Von Domarus's principle, I pointed out that what is subject and what is predicate are not building blocks of experience but are themselves the result of experience. When a patient has experienced a characteristic of a person as being more fundamental, more lasting, more "identical" than the person as a whole, this characteristic acquires qualities of the subject, and the person, then merely a personification of this more stable idea, acquires qualities of the predicate. Here "blue eyedness" had acquired the qualities of a subject. This phenomenon also appeared in the patient cited in chapter 2 for whom having Heidi-like characteristics was much more important and more stable than being the same person. As I commented earlier, such stability can be thought of in terms of Klüver's "subjectively equivalent stimuli."

Clinicians commonly talk about the concreteness of schizophrenic thought, but we also know that some schizophrenic patients can deal most effectively with subject matter on a very abstract level. A patient dealing with highly complex and abstract modern musical scales and notations comes to mind. One advantage of my radical formulation of the nature of the schizophrenic's objects is that it can accommodate both the very concrete and the very abstract.

Experienced clinicians make corrections when they note projective elements in their theory building. Many of us who have worked intensively for a long time with schizophrenic patients and are keenly aware of the limitations of our theoretical understanding of the disorder are constantly forced to look anew at phenomenology. In the face of clinical data, we are able to make shifts in our theoretical framework. Nevertheless, at any one point, every therapist operates with an explicit or implicit model for the disorder he treats. He may gradually formulate parts of the model with some precision but neglect or only vaguely sketch others. I would like to describe the parts of the model for which I have developed fairly precise ideas during my work with schizophrenic patients and the treatment strategies with which I think they are connected. I recognize, however, that the heuristic value of the treatment strategies is not necessarily dependent on the correctness of the proposed model.

Every dynamically oriented therapist who has written about schizophrenia—and even many who are not so oriented—has had to address the problem of boundaries between self (or self-object) and others, between inside and outside, and between objects. These issues, which at first glance are conceptualized spatially, move to the temporal dimension when we speak of the problem of object constancy. It is particularly in my work with schizophrenic patients, for whom the problem of (temporal) object constancy is so crucial, that I have experienced dissatisfaction with the reification connected with the spatial emphasis.

The central element in my formulation concerns perceptual theory, as it can and must be integrated into psychoanalytic thinking. The hypothesis that each perceptual act recapitulates the ontogeny of perception is central to ideas about schizophrenic thought disorder (Kafka, 1964, 1977). I have previously referred to Stein's experimental finding (1949) when he presented Rorschach cards tachistoscopically for only a small fraction of a second to adult subjects. When asked what they saw, some responded at first that it was only a flash. When urged to say more, subjects gave responses that resembled those of very young children. They might, for instance, say, "some red going up," the words accompanied by a gesture indicating the direction.

More recent and extensive related experimental work on per-

ception by a group at the University of Lund (Smith and Danielsson, 1982; Westerlundh and Smith, 1983) demonstrates beautifully that psychoanalytic concepts are essential for understanding
experimental findings in this area. Their meta-contrast technique
involves the tachistoscopic presentation of paired stimuli: incon-
gruent stimuli in one series, and the image of a threatening face
implying danger to the image of a young person in another series.
During one developmental phase, children close their own eyes
when they see a threatening face. During a subsequent developmental phase, they perceive the image of the threatened young
person as shutting *its* eyes. Among the defensive reactions that can
be measured in this complex work are repression, isolation, projection, and discontinuity. Repression, for instance, is scored if the
subject reports seeing a lifeless mask instead of a live threatening
face. Short exposures in "percept-genesis" tests reflect ontogenet-
ically early functional levels of the perceiver; reports after longer
exposure reflect the subject's present functional state. The Lund
workers point out how much perception has been neglected by
psychoanalytic writers because of the strong and persistent influence in psychoanalysis of the concept that perception simply "mir-
rors" reality. They show how a psychoanalytic understanding of
defensive operations in perceptual acts facilitates the understanding of their findings (see also Sandler and Rosenblatt, 1962; Sandler and Joffe, 1967).

I want to move now from ontogenetical recapitulation in perception to the related idea of object constancies derived from the
subjective equivalence of stimulus patterns that are similar but not
identical. For those who might charge that such a conceptualization of object constancy is too narrowly cognitive, I reemphasize
that the stimuli we select from an external and internal environment that we scan continuously, the stimuli that form the bases of
our constant objects, are chosen because of currently active drives,
needs, emotions, and moods of varying intensity, and the compromises between conflicting drives.

When focusing on schizophrenia, one must remember that a
perceptual act can be carried to relative completion, or it can be
stopped or interrupted before completion. If all perceptual acts are
carried to relative completion, the objects that are subjectively

equivalent at the end of the perceptual acts are the constant objects, as this term is used in general psychology, and cannot be dispensed with in psychoanalysis—where, however, the memory of the absent object is often emphasized. In any case, the constant object of consensually validated reality can be a constant table or a constant person. But we may postulate that rapidly fluctuating patterns of intense drives, resulting in a predominance of partial perceptual acts or mixtures of partial and completed perceptual acts, characterize the perceptual world of the schizophrenic patient. Normal object-constancy patterns thus either are disrupted or may never be fully established; instead, idiosyncratic schizophrenic constancies, based on the common denominators of partial and relatively completed perceptual acts, may be prominent in the patient's object world.

At the very center of my model of schizophrenic disorders is my understanding that recapitulative perceptual processes link affective and cognitive development. More accurately, these ideas occupy that part of the model about which I have been able to formulate specific and detailed ideas. Such a model may seem ambitious, but it is compatible with various competing hypotheses—psychoanalytic, psychodynamic, and biological—concerning the genetics of the rapidly fluctuating patterns of intense drives. Here my model is open or incomplete.

If the more constant objects are synonymous with highly idiosyncratic categories (for example, all family members with blue eyes or with a certain style of moving; all material objects with shiny surfaces; all friendly creatures and friendly material objects), the application of conventional logical thought processes to these objects will result in a thought disorder. Communication with the schizophrenic patient would indeed be impossible if there were no connection between the logical operations of doctor and patient. The notion of similar logic applied to different constant objects offers more hope if (1) techniques have been developed to study the patient's idiosyncratic objects, and (2) the therapist uses these techniques in learning how to become a relatively constant object in the patient's world.

Schematically, my major treatment strategy is connected to my proposed model of schizophrenic perceptions and object constancies. The therapist must suspend his commonsense notion of what constant objects are for the patient. A highly idiosyncratic characteristic may determine which objects are subjectively equivalent for the patient and thus constant for him or her. Once the therapist thoroughly suspends common sense concerning the nature of the patient's constant objects, but continues to apply the usual logical processes to the manipulation of the constancies that he detects, the patient may sense the therapist's empathy and experience it as the removal of a major obstacle to communication; on occasion he or she may be eager to teach the therapist something about his object world. (Dorothy L told me that she wanted to continue working with me despite the distance she had to travel to see me because it had taken her such a long time to train me.) The combination of suspended common sense in one area and its retention in another results in the therapist's multichannel communication pattern, a peculiar mixture of individually tailored crazy and sane talk. This kind of communication has the advantage of taking into account the rapidly shifting ego organizations of the patient. These shifts are often too rapid for the therapist to follow, but the chance of being on target sometimes is increased by the diversity of the approach.

Finally and most significantly, the therapist's multichannel presence facilitates the linkage of various characteristics of the therapist with the idiosyncratic network of characteristics underlying the patient's constancy patterns, thus facilitating the establishment of the therapist as a more constant object in the patient's world. (Dorothy L's hallucination of my recommendation that she enter a hospital is a case in point.) Only the therapist who has become a relatively constant object for the patient can have therapeutic leverage.

Chapter 6

The Individual and the Group: Rituals and Families

Ritual belongs at the center of some wider applications of my notions of multiple realities because ritual is associated with change (from one reality to another) and with the maintenance of continuity in the presence of change. The anthropologist is concerned with the place of rituals in rites of passage from one stage of life to another—birth, puberty, marriage, death—with rituals marking the change of seasons, and with those having to do with certain role changes, such as the establishment of authority—for instance, a coronation. Although the anthropologist does study individuals and individual families, his concern is usually with the nature of rites of passage in wider groups, such as specific tribes.

Rituals and "ritualistic behavior" are also, of course, of interest to the psychoanalytic therapist. The first part of this chapter is a rather abstract and theoretical examination—from the multiple-reality perspective—of ritual and ritualistic behavior. The second part deals more with clinical matters.

Examined in greater detail, ritual is at the center of the wider applications of my ideas of multiple realities because it is involved in the "rites of passage" between different realities as I have conceptualized them: the interconnected dichotomies of time-space, inner-outer (the size of the organism), and animate-inanimate, and their paradoxical coexistences. Since clinical practice permits a close look at and offers a special perspective on these reality organizations, a clinician who is interested in the integration of psychological, social, and cultural influences can contribute to the study of aspects of the behavior of the individual in groups, families, organizations, tribes, and ethnonational units.

Rituals and the Ritualistic

At first glance clinicians are more concerned with ritualistic behavior (it is a symptom) than with rituals, and anthropologists are more concerned with rituals proper. Both involve repetition. In a paper on repetition and the repetition compulsion, Hans Loewald (1971) makes the point that not all repetition is a manifestation of repetition compulsion. He elaborates the difference between a compelled tacit repetition and active repeating, working through what is being repeated. Loewald thus first makes a sharp distinction between two forms of repetition with which psychoanalysts are much concerned, the repetition compulsion, with the symptomatic overtones of the word *compulsion*, and "working through," with its curative connotations. In his paper "The Waning of the Oedipus Complex" (1979) he elaborates the idea that the same problematic is recurrent, not disposed of but reworked in different developmental stages and in the context of different life tasks. Here Loewald brings together again the two forms of repetition he had distinguished. The active reworking in different developmental stages and in the context of different life tasks is the working through that utilizes, is grafted onto, the compelled tacit repetition—I would say recapitulation—of the same problematic in the repetition compulsion. His distinction between and subsequent bringing together of repetition compulsion and working through are pertinent to the difference between and similarity of *ritualistic* and *ritual* because I see an analogy between his "compelled tacit repetition" and the inanimate as I have discussed it, and an analogy between his "active repeating, working through" and my "animate" center of action. From my perspective, however, an ongoing "reworking," recapitulation of perception is part of all the other processes that have to be re-worked. The psychoanalytically understood dynamics of the repe-tition compulsion apply to the microworld of perceptual processes.

Rituals can produce a feeling of completeness—a whole act, a finished sequence, the achievement (at least for a while) of satis-faction, satiation, perhaps serenity. But sometimes, as in ritualistic behavior, they may instead generate a feeling of mechanical repe-tition or the absence of a meaning achieved, the sense of being enmeshed in an endless series of aborted sequences. Both kinds of the behavior, the ritual and the ritualistic, emerge from a con-cern with boundaries, such as those between the individual and the group, what is within and what is without, the concrete or concretized-spatial and the psychological-temporal.

Ritual and the ritualistic address these divisions—which are central to our understanding of psychological reality—not con-sciously, perhaps, but in a particularly focused manner. My thesis is that both ritual and the ritualistic attempt to confirm and to challenge shared, commonsense, everyday reality by formalizing and dramatizing the divisions and the passages between these reality organizations. They attempt to confirm for the individual that he has roots in all these realities and that his rootedness in the ontogenetic and perhaps phylogenetic early ones does not cut him off from the later realities, including the commonsense reality essential for the performance of most daily tasks—the consen-sually validated reality based on similar degrees of completion of *perceptual acts*. Note that I specified that the ritual and the ritualis-tic both make the *attempt* to confirm the individual's rootedness in multiple realities, but I believe that ritual is relatively successful and that the ritualistic owes its mechanistic, driven repetitiveness to the fact that it is basically a failed ritual.

The rituals with which a psychoanalyst is concerned in daily clinical work are manifestations of obsessive-compulsive urges. Although the degree of ego dystonicity of such urges and acts may vary, they are often considered symptoms by the analysand and may be the overt reason an individual seeks psychoanalytic treat-ment. As work with the patient proceeds, however, the psycho-analyst may soon think of many other aspects of almost any patient's behavior as ritualistic. The way he enters the consultation room, a particular way of reclining on the couch, a manner of rising with a characteristic jerking or a slow rolling motion, his greetings or avoidance of greetings—these behaviors may have a ritualistic quality in the analyst's eyes, not recognized as such by the patient but eventually of importance in understanding him and in formulating interpretations. The extent to which such rituals can be seen as related to those which the anthropologist studies depends on the conceptualization of the nature of both kinds of ritual.

The analyst may be especially aware of the ritual component of behavior within a given society, both through contact with persons whose behavior does not conform to social norms and through a growing understanding of the personal dynamics of conformity. My own concept of the nature of ritual leads me to believe that despite some surface differences, the term *ritual* signifies the same fundamental characteristics to the clinician and the anthropologist (Kafka, 1983). Both fields understand the structural role of rituals as in some way related to the attempt to maintain the psychological homeostasis necessary for the individual's functioning in a social context.

In my view, the occurrence of rituals at such times as birth, puberty, marriage, and death derives from the basic stabilizing function of ritual in situations with the potential for instilling dystonic feelings ranging from discomfort to terror. Two major characteristics of cultural rites also emerge in clinical counterparts. One is a precision of performance of the ritual act, in which the emphasis on the concreteness of the ritual object (the preserved limb of the saint, the specific location of the pilgrimage) coexists with emphasis on an abstract symbolism—the nonconcrete mental or spiritual charge with which the ritual performance or event is invested. Thus, the ritual is a condensed encounter of material and psychological extremes, the concrete and the abstract polarities. (Recall my previous discussion of the material-spatial "equivalence" and the psychological-time "equivalence.") The second characteristic is ritual confrontation of the issue of the boundary of the individual and the relationships between the individual and the other, the inside and the outside (the depth of the *individual* commitment to the *bond* to the bride or groom, to the community of the religious order).

As I discussed earlier, in biology what is considered a unit is in some sense arbitrary. For example, it is unclear whether certain marine organisms should be considered colonies of unicellular organisms or individual animals. The anthropologist encounters the boundary question in the study of the rites of passage when the individual "becomes a part" of the society. The clinician frequently comes to understand rituals as connected with the patient's struggles to define or protect his own boundaries. Victor Turner is an anthropologist whose central concern is liminality (1977) and the rituals that serve as stabilizers when the anxiety is greatest, when one has left one condition and not yet entered another—the way to the altar, fertility rites, last rites. Perhaps Turner and other anthropologists with similar interests might agree that the rituals they study concern, first, such matters as transcendence of the concrete, the material, the body, and, second, the boundary between individual and societal entities.

Developments in modern physics that have made inroads on commonsense understanding of matter, energy, and time, no doubt contributing to the zeitgeist, play some role in contemporary explorations of perennial questions involving the linkage of the psychological and the temporal. I have emphasized how various authors who have approached this issue from very different angles have independently concluded that the study of mind and the study of time are intertwined. Hugh Longuet-Higgins (1968), a theoretician of communication and a mathematical model builder, proposes a model of the brain based on the model of the holograph, but he transforms the holograph by giving a temporal rather than a spatial meaning to the terms in the mathematical formulae describing its physics. In holography, each point in space has *some* information about all other points in space;[1] in the temporal analogue, each "point" in time has *some* information about every other point in time (past and future). Longuet-Higgins's treatment of the brain in temporal terms—rather than in commonsense, "material," concrete terms—perhaps brings us closest to Loewald's trenchant characterization of "time as . . . the inner fibre

---

1. If we cut the holographic picture of a man in half, we obtain not a picture of an upper half and one of a lower half, but two pictures of the whole man, although they are not as sharp as the original picture.

of what we call psychical" (1962, p. 268). Longuet-Higgins's
model clarifies our understanding of the unique qualities of the
human mind and human consciousness—awareness that each moment, although different from that which went before and that
which will follow, is rich with memory and with anticipation, with
retrospect and with prospect. Without this richness of time the
moment, the *psychological now*, loses its meaning. All "meaning" disappears if we empty "now" of memory and retrospect, of
prospect and anticipation.

A whole literature deals with the pathogenic consequences that
result when the *temporal* psychological event undergoes a transformation through reification, concretization, *spatialization*. Much of
this literature is summarized by Joseph Gabel in *La fausse conscience: Essai sur la réification* (1962). Here he develops the
theme that estrangement, common to ideology and schizophrenia,
is grounded in such reification, the spatialization of the temporal.
The "reification" of political ideology and of what he considers the
inherent "ideological" nature of schizophrenia have this in common: ideology is fixed, lifeless, unresponsive to outer and inner
life. Gabel's concept of ideology thus has a clearly negative connotation.

On the surface, but I believe only on the surface, this contrasts
with Erik Erikson's initially positive reference to the ideological
element, "the element providing a coherence of ideas and ideals"
which "become part of formal rites" in the ontogeny of ritualization (1966, p. 617). Erikson says that only after the addition of the
ideological element "can man be said to be adult in the sense that
he can devote himself to ritual purposes and eventually be trusted
to become the '*everyday ritualizer*' in his children's life" (p. 617;
italics mine). The "everyday ritualizer" is also the socializer.

Erikson starts out by studying human ritualization in contrast
and in relation to animal ritualization as described by the etholo-
gist. His positive evaluation of ritual derives from its roots in the
mother-infant recognition, such as the appreciation conveyed by a
greeting, which fosters a sense of self in the infant and helps
maintain it in the mother. He introduces a more negative element
when he discusses human ritualization as largely related to the
existence of human "pseudo-species"—tribes, clans, classes—

which consider all outsiders as enemies, and he foresees the possibility that humanity will succeed in diminishing its pseudo-species divisiveness. I believe that for Erikson ideology thus also implies a certain concretization. The positive aspects of Erikson's evaluation of the ideological result not so much from a view of ideology essentially different from Gabel's as from the position that at our current state of development, roots in a somewhat concretized group must to some extent coexist with individualism that would otherwise risk being autistic. Such dialectic conflicts are characteristic of all the developmental phases described by Erikson.

Here we meet again an untenable commonsense idea—we cannot take it for granted that the size of an organism is an absolute given. It is not only in marine organisms that it is fundamentally unclear whether a unit of a given size is a colony of unicellular organisms or a whole animal. Essential ambiguities for such complex animals as human beings arise from the person's functioning as an individual and at the same time as member of a dyad (mother-infant, for instance) and as member of a larger group. Since I believe that current prominent attempts in psychoanalysis to distinguish "self" from "ego" represent an effort to do away with an essential ambiguity on the intraindividual level, a discussion of them is relevant at this point.

In self psychology, which attempts to clarify issues related to the experiencing or self-representations of the image of the self, Kohut's (1971) name is currently in the foreground. Freud's ambiguous usage of "Das Ich" is often critically cited in this connection. Although the concept of self-representation is clinically useful, I believe that on a more theoretical level the ego-self differentiation can be a pseudosolution—that is, it can gloss over a problem that is more interesting if its unsolved paradoxical nature is faced squarely. In their discussion of *ego*, Laplanche and Pontalis mention the history of the usage of "Ich" in psychoanalysis and the conceptual problems involved:

> Some authors have sought, for the sake of clarity, to make a conceptual distinction between the ego as agency, as substructure of the personality, and the ego as love-object for the individual himself. . . . Hartmann, for example, has suggested a way of get-

ting rid of the ambiguity which arises in his view from the use of terms such as "narcissism" and "ego-cathexis" (Ich-Besetzung). . . . in using the term narcissism, two different sets of opposites often seem to be fused into one. The one refers to the self (one's own person) in contradistinction to the object, the second to the ego (as a psychic system) in contradistinction to the other sub-structures of personality. However, the opposite of object cathexis is not ego cathexis, but cathexis of one's own person, that is, self-cathexis; in speaking of self-cathexis we do not imply whether this cathexis is situated in the id, in the ego, or in the superego. . . . It therefore will be clarifying if we define narcissism as the libidinal cathexis not of the ego but of the self. (1967, p. 131)

Laplanche and Pontalis go on to say:

In our view this position builds upon a purely conceptual distinction, running ahead of a real solution to some essential problems. The danger of proposing a usage of "Ich" which is taken to be exclusively psycho-analytical by contrast with other more traditional senses is that the real contributions of the Freudian usage may be lost. For Freud *exploits* traditional usages: he opposes organism to environment, subject to object, internal to external, and so on, while continuing to employ "Ich" at these different levels. What is more, he plays on the ambiguities thus created, so that none of the connotation normally attaching to "ego" or "I" ("Ich") is forgotten. It is this complexity that is shunned by those who want a different word. (pp. 131–32)

Although there is ambiguity in the idea of self-observation, it is the concreteness and spatialization of a self-observing self that make the ambiguity so difficult and motivate those who want to eliminate it. I believe that the advantages of the Freudian ambiguity, which Laplanche and Pontalis also want to preserve, lie in its avoidance of a one-sided concretization (of "Ich"), which is essentially spatial and incompatible with my gropings for a new understanding of psychological reality—an understanding that has already achieved distance from common sense in recognizing time as the "fiber of mind," basically a mind-time equation. A self-ego dichotomy freezes the situation (and I admit that such freezing may at times have clinical value and may permit a useful "look" at some self-representations) and does not easily accommodate the previously developed notion of "animation" into a center of autonomous action.

The rituals observed by clinicians and anthropologists both have essentially a reality-anchoring function. For example, when Erikson discusses the recognition-greeting ritual of mother and infant, he emphasizes the formation of the individual's sense of his own existence and of a reality that, through generational "cog-wheeling" (Erikson using David Rapaport's phrase)—that is, the transmission of meaning and values from one generation to the next—links it to the reality of the group. This recognition-greeting ritual thus deals with the inside-outside (size of the group) dimension of the perceptual recapitulation. And once again I must summarize my central thesis: perceptual recapitulation of the ontogeny of perception is the basis for the establishment of object constancies. Scanning implies a temporal dimension, and motivational intensity (hunger, for instance) influences scanning speed. Furthermore, time experiences—time sensations and judgments—are profoundly affected by drive states and affects. Time judgments are based on *subjectively equivalent temporal intervals*, and dominant affects and moods determine the selection of the reference interval. My emphasis on the importance of the ever-contracting and ever-expanding temporal grids of psychic activity is in harmony with such authors as Gabel, who contrasts the temporal fluidity of psychological processes with "alienating," essentially nonpsychological, concretization and spatialization.

We are here again dealing with the difficult equation of the most "pure" psychological processes with temporal processes. Our practical need to deal with a concrete reality persists in reinforcing our resistance against the mind-time translation. Facing this difficulty permits us to make explicit a feature that is implicit in some of Erikson's remarks on developmental ritualization. As has been mentioned, Erikson links a necessary ritualization (to avoid autism) that is part of generational cog-wheeling to the development of a feeling of belonging to groups, clans, and other human pseudo-species. In Gabel's terms, the operational concreteness implied by Erikson's pseudo-species would be seen as psychologically "false" in a very specific sense, for Gabel considers projection of "bad aspects of myself" feelings as spatialization of the psychological (temporal). I will show below that when Erikson relates ritual to the basic individual-group dichotomy, the structure

of this dichotomy is similar to that of the psychological-concrete
(temporal-spatial) dichotomy as discussed by Gabel.

If the ritual's concern with the individual-group boundary also
means a concern with the boundary of the psychological (temporal) and concretized (spatial), questions of ambiguity on one
border correspond to the same questions on the other. Erikson
discusses ambiguity as it relates to ritualization, to self and other,
to individual and group. In summarizing basic elements of ritualization (starting with the greeting-recognition of mother and infant) he says:

> Its mutuality is based on the *reciprocal* needs of two quite
> *unequal* organisms and minds; yet, it unites them in *practical
> reality* as well as in *symbolic actuality*. It is a highly *personal*
> matter, and is yet *group-bound*; by the same token it heightens a
> sense both of *belongingness* and of personal *distinctiveness*. It is
> *playful*, and yet *formalized*, and this in *details* as well as in the
> whole *procedure*. Becoming *familiar* through repetition, it yet
> renews the *surprise* of recognition which provides a catharsis of
> affects. And while the ethologists will tell us that ritualization in
> the animal world must, above all, provide an *unambiguous* set of
> signals so as to avoid fatal misunderstanding, we suspect that in
> man, the *overcoming of ambivalence* is an important aim of such
> ritualization. (1966, p. 605; Erikson's italics)

Before examining some problems in Erikson's text, let us take
a closer look at the juxtaposed topics of ambiguity and ambivalence. Since ambivalence refers to good and bad feelings toward
the same object, it takes for granted an antecedent degree of object
constancy, a certain solidity (concreteness) of the borders of the
self, a solidity of the boundary between inside and outside. The
formal logical structure of ambiguity, as discussed in chapter 2, is
pertinent here, as is the finding, on a more clinical level, that
parental fear of ambiguity may be a pathogenic element leading
the offspring to experience estrangement and alienation when
confronted with the ineluctable ambiguities and paradoxes of life.

With those points in mind, let us return to Erikson's emphasis
on the relationship, in ritualization in animals and man, between
the need for an *unambiguous* set of signals and the *overcoming of
ambivalence*. Recall that in order to tolerate the infant's first step,
the mother must for the briefest moment have the delusion that the

infant will not fall. This delusion occurs at a moment of psychological lack of separation of the two individuals involved. In a sense, it is the mother's ability to laugh at herself and her delusion when the fall occurs but has no serious injurious consequences that permits the infant's further development. I would now add that it is this delusion that permits the mother, for a moment, to give an unambiguous set of signals that the first step should be attempted. The signal is unambiguous at the moment when the definition of the individual is ambiguous, when the boundaries between mother and infant are blurred. (It should also be noted here that psychoanalytic theory offers a conceptual bridge between ambivalence and the ambiguity about what unit is in the mother-infant dyad. Since the infant equates good with the satisfaction of his needs and bad with the lack of satisfaction—that is, with *need*, something he cannot himself satisfy—the differentiation of inner and outer in a sense corresponds to the birth of good and bad.) It is the phase-appropriate degree of ease with which the mother can cross the fusion-differentiation (from her infant) barrier that indeed forms the foundation of what Erikson calls "*the overcoming of ambivalence*," which is "an important aim of . . . ritualization."

While "the overcoming of ambivalence" is a term that succeeds in conveying a readiness to act, it is somewhat misleading. Ambivalence is not "overcome," it is tolerated. The distinction is important because "overcoming" sets up false expectations. Erikson himself writes:

> What we love or admire is also threatening, awe becomes awfulness. . . . Therefore, ritualized affirmation, at first playfully improvised, becomes indispensable as a periodical experience and must find new forms in the context of new development actualities. Its perversion or absence, in turn, leaves a sense of dread or impoverishment. . . . the earliest affirmation soon becomes reaffirmation in the face of the fact that the very experiences by which man derives a measure of familiarity also expose him to a series of estrangements. The first of these is a sense of separation by abandonment to which corresponds, on the part of the mother, a chilling sense of not being needed; both must be prevented by the persistent, periodical reassurance of familiarity and mutuality. (p. 605)

Of course, the separation does and must occur, but I agree with Erikson that the earliest affirmation persists in the recurrent ritual. But the ritual, because it represents the extreme confrontation of the concrete, precisely defined, individually bordered spatial on the one hand and the boundary-loosened, psychological, temporal on the other also is the periodic recurrence of the beginning—of the first (tolerated) step.

Elements of the ritual and the ritualistic, thus conceived, are pervasive if not omnipresent. When clinicians and anthropologists have a closer look at the rituals traditionally studied by each other's discipline, the similarities of the structural-qualitative characteristics of ritual become more obvious, and the differences are more likely to be seen in quantitative terms. In all rituals the time-mind-communal/space-concrete-individual ambiguities are not "overcome," but individuals vary in their degree of tolerance of the tensions at the border and therefore in the frequency and manner in which they either must immerse themselves in the experience of a wide or paradoxical reality or must *ritualistically* defend against such immersion. Rituals also vary in the manner in which they deal with the time-mind-communal/space-concrete-individual tensions and ambiguities. More specifically, the polarity-tension that is the raison d'être and the core structure of rituals also manifests itself in the evolution of ritual.

To illustrate the broader application of these ideas, an example from religious ritual. With the destruction of the Second Temple and the exodus to Babylon, a significant evolution occurred in the spiritualization of Jewish ritual, which became freed from attachment to concrete sacrifice at a concrete and exclusive site, the Temple in Jerusalem. Judaism became a portable religion of the word (Graetz, 1893). Yet the tension persists in Jewish worship, and the counterforce of the concrete polarity always manifests itself again in those aspects of the concretization of words and ideas that Gabel considers when he discusses "ideology" (Gabel, 1967). Although the concrete site and the concrete sacrifice may be missing, Jewish orthodox ritual insists on the importance of the defined, the circumscribed—for example, the right prayer at the right time, the correct garment, and the yarmulkah. The abstract, the psychological, is again pulled toward concretization, a kind of primitivization of religious ritual.

The tensions in religious groups between traditionalists clinging to more concrete formalities and those who want to deemphasize them in favor of the spiritual and ideational are always close to the surface. I do not want to use the word *ideological* because of the loading of concreteness that Gabel gives it, but my very avoidance of it reflects the ease with which there is always the "return of the concrete," analogous to the "return of the repressed" of the psychoanalyst. In the evolution of ritual, what is at any one moment considered acceptable is that which is perceived as essentially a subjective equivalent to a former ritual; its repetition reinforces a particular system of equivalences and anchors a view of reality, such as a specific myth of creation. It also serves as a defense against other views of reality.

Clinicians are familiar with such phenomena since patients' rituals can also serve both as an anchor for one reality and as a defense against other views of reality. A vast literature of psychopathology deals with the concrete thinking of schizophrenic patients (Gabel cites much of it). Clinicians who are familiar with this literature are sometimes puzzled by the high-level abstraction manifested by some schizophrenic patients in such areas as mathematics, theory of harmony, and musical composition. As I emphasized in the previous chapter, descriptions of the schizophrenic's objects as either concrete or abstract do not do them justice. Schizophrenics' object constancies, resulting from the mixture of completed and arrested perceptual acts, are idiosyncratic and are sometimes both very concrete and very abstract. ("Heidi-ness" was more constant than any one individual.) The schizophrenics' objects can thus resemble ritual objects, which have a particularly heavy abstract-symbolic *and* concrete-specific loading. While from one perspective Dorothy L, the patient with the reality-anchoring "Heidi-ness" image, was *apparently* involved with an abstraction, she also manifested behavior illustrating schizophrenic concreteness. During one schizophrenic episode she strictly observed a personal taboo that can be understood as a negative ritual. The psychiatrist who was administrator of her hospital unit emphasized patients' personal grooming. If prior to their hospitalization they had gone to a beauty shop once a week, they were urged to do so during their hospitalization. If a patient had shaved her legs at home, she was urged to do so in the hospital. Dorothy L refused to do so, saying she had her "father's legs." In effect, she was asserting a view of reality in which she was not separate from, and controlled parts of, her deceased father. As she emerged from the schizophrenic episode, rituals of adoration of her father took more conventional forms, such as walks in places and at times corresponding to his preferences.

In the usual psychoanalytic work with neurotic patients, the "blinder" functions of ritualistic behavior are the most readily observable in the consulting room. For example, ritualistic repetitions of ways of moving avoid body sensations that are threatening because of unconscious erotic wishes toward the analyst or because they would too easily lead—in unconscious fantasy that is eventually uncovered—to an aggressive act or gesture. Rituals in the consulting room also seem related to phase-specific drives and defenses against them; the ritualistic behavior often seems to be a manifestation of a compromise in this area. More descriptively, certain ritualistically maintained rigidities literally act as blinders. For example, a patient may not be able to look at a painting in the analyst's office because it does not match her view of the analyst's characteristics, a view that she has to maintain and that is consistent with the current stage of transference development.

The idiosyncrasy and repetitiveness of some behavior, its stilted and desiccated characteristics, may lead the clinician to think of it as ritualistic, but it is difficult to draw a line distinguishing it sharply from other symptomatic behavior. The isolation of affect may be particularly striking in behavior that therapists are inclined to label ritualistic because the "dramatic elaboration" (Erikson, p. 614) of the sequence is in such marked contrast to the apparent mechanical nature of the performance. In the clinical setting, what is called ritualistic is often *desiccated drama*. Mr. Brown, the patient mentioned in chapter 1 who moved back and forth between mistress and wife during his analysis, did so in a manner that could be described as desiccated drama. The moves were accompanied by loud dramatic scenes, but they had a pseudoaffective, compulsive, and mechanistic quality. The insight that the moves had something to do with his adoptive parents and his idealized natural parents eventually led to a marked diminution of this particular desiccated drama, to a decrease in ritualistic-manneristic behavior generally, and to an increased sense of continuity in his life and in his relationships. The difficulty of distinguishing the ritualistic from the impulse-defense compromises that are labeled symptomatic behavior—or simply from other behavior, since all socialized behavior contains at least a component of such a symptomlike compromise—lies in the fact that it is only quantitatively more dramatic and more desiccated. Ritual as I conceptualize it, rooted in time-space dualities, saturates human activities and existence.

If ritual has a reality-anchoring function, its ubiquity is no surprise, but what have we gained by this formulation? And how is the desiccated drama of ritualistic behavior in the consulting room related to ecstatic ritual? In one analytic session, a patient experienced some loosening of desiccated drama, isolated affect had begun to acknowledge its object, and he had experienced a sense of greater freedom and autonomy. Afterward he found himself laughing at his own sudden thought while he was waiting on a subway platform. Experiencing a lightening of the psychological weight he carried, he thought, "Even living and dying are not a matter of life and death." This experience, I believe, contained the essence of the successful ritual—a breaking out from the ritualistic. Although this analysand did not consciously at this moment see himself as a member of a larger group, a link in a generational chain, the lightening he experienced involved a diminution of his sense of isolation, an implicit increase in the sense of connectedness to the rest of humanity. This is what the ritualistic tries for and what the ritual occasionally achieves. It may be that the more complete the achievement, the less often it *must* be reexperienced, and the less successful, the more it must automatically be repeated in dry ritualistic attempts.

The laughing experience that living and dying may not be so serious—not a "matter of life and death"—has some analogy to the mother-infant fusion in which the mother has the delusion that the infant will not fall when he takes the first step. The analysand's sudden laughter on encountering his liberating thought is also reminiscent of Erikson's *"surprise* of recognition which provides a catharsis of affects" (p. 605; Erikson's italics), an element in the earliest ritualization which starts in the mother-infant greeting and recognition.

Through the recapitulative nature of our affectively informed, drive-determined perceptual processes, we continually traverse multiple realities—which may be characterized by confusion or separation of the inner and outer, the animate and inanimate, or time and space—toward a consensually validated commonsense reality. Rituals, in a sense, give public and dramatic recognition to these ongoing individual voyages, which are usually not conscious and generally private. We are only too familiar with the danger of rituals when they validate and value "regressive" primitive reality organizations. Formulations emphasizing the delegation of super-ego functions and descriptions of projective and introjective phe-nomena in the rituals of a Nazi rally, for instance, must be sup-plemented by an examination of the corresponding perceptual "distortions" or different "reality organizations" in such situa-tions. The role of drugs in rituals—such as mescaline in religious rites of some Native American groups—illustrates recognition of the importance of experiencing dramatically and publicly passage through multiple-reality organizations.

Ritual confirms and sustains everyday reality *by* challenging it in the sense of evoking the prior realities traversed in the evolution of the current one. Its historicity made apparent, everyday reality is imbued with life. Ernst Kris's well-known phrase "regression in the service of the ego" (1952) relates to the freedom, so essential for any creativity, to travel in ascending and descending directions along this recapitulative path. Successful rituals permit and foster in institutionally sanctioned ways the questioning of any one real-ity, the widest possible travel along this recapitulative pathway. The patterns of subjective equivalence along this path, however, may include some which represent "realities" that for personal developmental reasons are particularly conflict-laden, which cor-respond to neurotic fixation points. The abortive nature of ritualis-tic behavior is related to those fixation points, and successful analytic treatment thus transforms the ritualistic into the possibility of successful, enriching, perhaps even ecstatic ritual of an anchoring in an enhanced reality that incorporates the rediscovery of one's development.

In recent decades performance art has introduced the private ritual into a public forum. It is an arena in which it is particularly difficult to separate the ritualistic from ritual. There is no question, however, that the performed rituals of some artists demonstrate rather well the multiple-reality organizations that I have outlined. The performance artist is an individual whose public performances of private ritual are intended to make a statement about who he or she is. Sometimes the performed ritual is also designed as a condensed statement about the personal development of the artist, the genesis of protest, of attitudes and beliefs, about the acceptance (or, more commonly, the rejection) of societal values. The oeuvre of the well-known German artist Beuys, his "rituals" (one can imagine a performance consisting of his standing on a chair in an empty room, wearing a bowler hat and shattering a piece of glass), can be understood as a statement of his need for "ritualization" despite Beuys's disillusionment—in the post-Nazi period— with the meaning of the rituals of all social units: family, religious, and national groups. The ritualization that Beuys has in mind, the personal act, despite its "autistic" character, is intended to be a celebration which we associate ordinarily with formal religious or nonreligious solemnity.

Whether or not we accept such a self-consciously autistic performance as art, the very designation of an individual act with presumably only personal meaning as a ritual (not a ritualistic symptom) strikes us as peculiar—as it is intended to do—and underscores that *ordinarily* rituals are group-related. Rituals may or may not be performed in groups—although there is usually a preference for their performance in a group (the minyan of the Jewish service, for example)—but even the ritual carried out individually indicates concern with, usually adherence to, and, for the performance artist, focused protest against the values or beliefs of the group. The group concerns are of course most clearly illustrated by rituals that mark the entry of the individual into the group (coming-of-age ceremonies), the acceptance of the institution sanctioned by the group (marriage), and the founding of the family.

So far, in our theoretical and rather abstract examination of ritual, the boundary between the individual and the larger social unit occupies a prominent place. The family is the social unit that has received the most careful clinical scrutiny, and it is in the work with a family that its characteristic rituals are most visible to the clinician.

The Patient in the Family

In this chapter, I have endeavored to relate a prominent manifestation of group life, the ritual, to what I have learned in individual analytic treatment about the organization of multiple realities. Because the size of the organism is itself one of the fluctuating elements in the realities under consideration, the term *individual treatment* can also be seen from an enlarged perspective, one that could be conceptualized as a kind of analytically informed systems theory. In discussing the connection between theory and clinical practice, I have thus far focused largely on individual treatment. The connection between theory and clinical practice, however, can also be illustrated in family therapy. For those who specialize in family therapy, there has been a gradual shift away from emphasis on mental illness as a characteristic of the individual to the view that disturbance in one family member is a symptom of the functioning of the entire family. Regardless of whether one adopts that explanatory position, specific aspects of family dynamics are of practical importance in the intensive psychoanalytically oriented treatment of the hospitalized patient whose treatment can be interrupted by the family.

It is commonly said that a patient is often removed from therapy when his improvement threatens to upset the family equilibrium or to lead to the revelation of family secrets. Some family studies concentrate more on the etiologic importance of family dynamics in the development of specific psychopathological pictures (see Lidz and Fleck, 1960; Wynne et al., 1958). Other investigators have emphasized therapeutic aspects of family work (for example, Ackerman, 1963) or both therapy and etiology (Bowen, 1961).

The approach to work with families that will be described here developed gradually in a private psychoanalytically oriented hospital in which all patients receive intensive individual therapy and the patient population comprises a large proportion of chronic schizophrenics. A schematic history of the evolution of work with families in this setting follows.

Initially, the hospital administrators believed that the patient had to be protected from his family, and vice versa. The family, however, had to be sufficiently informed about the patient to continue their financial and other support of the treatment. Another traditional function of the work with families was the use of family members as sources of historical material. Although the patient's therapist, the clinical administrator, and other hospital staff members saw the family occasionally, this function was carried on primarily by the social worker. More intense contact with the family usually occurred in connection with some crisis in the life of the patient or another family member.

As work with the family began to evolve, the emphasis shifted to more detailed and direct study of the family interaction during visits to the hospital plus some direct observation in the family home. The evolving flexible approach was founded on the recognition that although intensive individual psychotherapy remained the major therapeutic tool, a number of group approaches and milieu therapy could be usefully combined with it. The techniques I will describe developed in a setting in which the salient psychoanalytic therapy was performed by highly individualistic therapists, the functions of the individual therapist and the clinical administrator were usually performed by two different psychiatrists, and the clinical administrators of different units had varying philosophies and styles of administration, which meant that they had widely diverging techniques of dealing with families.

The nature of the setting, the patient population, the distance many families lived from the hospital, and the focus on individual treatment all contributed to the development of an extremely flexible way of working with families. In contrast to family therapy as it is often practiced, we did not adopt the stance of considering the entire family as the patient. Despite our frequent recognition of mutually deviant relationships, one hospitalized person was identified as the patient. In what can already be called traditional family therapy, family meetings with the therapist usually constitute the only therapy for all family members, and there is no one designated patient. In our hospital situation there was a designated patient who was primarily in intensive, individual, psychoanalytically oriented therapy. In traditional family therapy, "the family" is defined at the beginning of treatment. In our work, "the family" was an open-ended concept that could gradually expand to include more peripheral members. In another contrast to the usual family approaches, we did not require all members to come to all sessions; rather, the occurrence and avoidance of particular combinations of family members often had a ritualized rigidity. These fixed patterns were studied as possible indicators of patterns of family dynamics; combinations avoided by the family might be specifically encouraged and attempts made to disrupt the stereotyped and ritualized communication between family members apparently chosen to maintain the status quo.

Instead of structuring the family sessions in terms of length, number, and point of termination, we permitted flexibility in this area, too, with the amount of family involvement perhaps diminishing as the patient progressed toward discharge from the hospital and often toward the status of private patient of his hospital therapist. Instead of insisting, as family therapy usually does, that all information given by family members be shared, "confidential" data given by the identified patient—but not by his or her relatives—could be accepted by the therapist, although the whole family usually shared uncovered data eventually. Instead of the common practice of having one family therapist for the duration of the treatment, we permitted a change if circumstances made that necessary or desirable. For example, in the course of one patient's hospitalization, a social worker and the clinical administrator in effect took turns having the most active contact with the family during various phases of treatment. It must be emphasized, however, that because the staff of the hospital had an extremely low turnover, any staff member who had met members of the family— the individual therapist, the psychiatric social worker, the clinical

administrator, and occasionally nursing and activities personnel—
could usually be brought into family meetings when this was
clinically indicated.

The single most important technical aspect of this work as it
developed was the fact that there were meetings of many different
combinations of family and staff members. Frequently, the staff
made explicit plans concerning the composition of the meetings,
and the question of who met whom was itself studied in terms of its
dynamic implications. We learned that the tendencies to avoid
certain groupings were consistent inside and outside the hospital.
It was remarkable how long such patterns could go unnoticed by
both the family and the hospital staff until the staff began to focus
specifically on the study of such avoidance. In one family, for
example, only after several years of work—during which almost
all combinations of family members had been seen together—did
the staff notice that the patient and her father had never been seen
without the presence of another family member; this datum took
on special significance in the light of considerable clinical evidence, both from individual and from family therapy, that prior to
hospitalization, periods during which father and daughter were
alone with each other had been particularly traumatic.

Brody and Hayden (1957) have observed that the intrateam
reactions in a clinic may be a reduplication, diminished in intensity, of the significant family conflicts. These observations were
confirmed in our setting, and our permissiveness toward the development of multiple combinations permitted us to observe the
parallelism of patterns of avoidance within the family and within
the hospital staff. For example, in one situation where the father
was ignored by the mother and the patient, the administrator
seldom met with the social worker and the therapist. Furthermore,
we noted that a family in which the internal power structure was
being tested by the family members might also test the power
structure of the hospital staff in a parallel way. For instance, a
family in which the father's power was being questioned repeatedly tested whether or not the medical director of the hospital
would overrule the decision of the unit administrator. When members of the hospital's administrative hierarchy were informed of
this family pattern, the resulting changed approach interrupted the

family's long-established pattern of moving the patient from one institution to another after brief hospitalizations.

Our study of which combinations of individuals were being formed, dissolved, or avoided also led to an unexpected finding about staff functioning. We did not consistently find that all families attempted to remove the patient when his or her improvement threatened the family equilibrium. Sometimes there seemed to be unconscious collusion between the therapist and family members to take the patient out of the hospital at a time of positive transference. The therapist then blamed the family for the interruption of treatment during a period of apparent improvement. But when our family work reversed the situation and the patient remained in the hospital, the short-lived transference improvement often disappeared; therapists were not always grateful for the work with the families that had thus exposed the incomplete treatment.

One variant of the multiple-combination technique consisted of deliberately introducing a peripheral family member or friend into one of the family meetings, particularly when a patient's apparently psychotic communication in individual therapy had indicated that the peripheral individual was "different"—that is, less fused with other family members. It was our experience that such an individual was likely to reveal a family secret. For example, a visiting aunt, described in the patient's obscure communications as separate from the family, revealed in one session what eight closer relatives had not mentioned in many visits extending over almost five years—namely, that the patient's mother had exerted formidable control over the family by repeatedly and convincingly threatening suicide.

Often the patient's communications about his family made no sense if we dealt only with the manifest family as it presented itself to the hospital. Our techniques can be seen as attempts to reach the latent elements behind the manifest façade. There are three ways in which the term *latent* can be used in reference to family work. First, it can be used to designate the potential strength of the family, which is expected to emerge if the goals of therapy are achieved. The second meaning is closely related to Murray Bowen's conceptualization concerning the gradually emerging chiefs of a clan, which he presented at a Georgetown University symposium on schizophrenia in 1961. A new chief emerges only when the limits of the old chief's tolerance are reached. The practical task of discovering who in the family can really decide whether or not hospitalization can be supported, financially and otherwise, had long sensitized us to the emergence of the hidden chiefs of the clan. For example, the husband, manifest head of the family, says, "We cannot afford her hospitalization here." At this point, an apparently peripheral uncle-in-law says quietly, "Well, let's have another look at that question later." The atmosphere changes, and clinical matters relating to hospitalization are then discussed.

The third meaning of *latent* refers to idiosyncratic relationships within the family that are not visible on the surface. Our emphasis on this third meaning is related to the observation, in the individual psychotherapy of psychotics in our setting, that the language of schizophrenic patients often reveals and sometimes deals almost exclusively with specific themes of the family mythology. Mrs. W often referred to murderers or killers. She fostered the clinical impression that she hallucinated the voice of her mother and, shortly thereafter, the voice of her sister. We gradually learned, however, that, strictly speaking, neither the mother's nor the sister's voice was hallucinated. In earlier chapters I have pointed out that for a psychotic patient, characteristics of someone may be more stable than the individual. For Mrs. W a perceived characteristic of both the mother and the sister had more stability than either person. This characteristic derived from a prominent theme in the family myth with which Mrs. W was concerned. She believed that there were killers in the family. The parents had decided, after many consultations, that a sibling of the patient should have surgery. When the child died during the surgery, the mother, whom Mrs. W held responsible for the decision, became classified by her as a "killer." Further, a category of "killers in the family" was established in her mind. All those who were considered "killers" were subjectively equivalent to each other, not differentiated from each other. Her mother and sister were subjectively equivalent when the patient was concerned with the killer theme. At one point in therapy, she wondered if she herself was a killer, too.

On the other hand, when she was concerned with the theme of physical appearance, Mrs. W was quite sure that she, brown-eyed and dark-haired, was separate from her sister and mother, both blue-eyed and blonde. Her sister and mother were subjectively equivalent whenever she talked about physical appearance. When she was concerned with the theme of the friendly ones in the family, those who were "warm and make easy contacts," then she and her mother, but not her sister, were subjectively equivalent. Besides the manifest family—the brothers, sisters, husbands, and parents whom the hospital staff meets—there exists in a patient's mind a series of latent families which depends on the context activated in treatment. For the patient different family members may be fused into one if a common characteristic makes them subjectively equivalent. The multiple-reality concept has direct clinical application here. Thus, when patient and family are seen in a variety of combinations, the patient who is concerned with certain basic themes can be helped to form and maintain increasingly stable identities of person as opposed to identities of theme. For example, after a series of multiple-combination family sessions, this patient could sort out identities, saying: "I'm different from you, Mother. I don't kill and I have a nicer figure. You can't even drive a car."

The flexible approach to work with families can thus contribute to increasingly stable feelings of identity in the hospitalized patient. The techniques I have described may also permit the family to tolerate shifts in its equilibrium related to the treatment of the hospitalized member. Premature termination of treatment may thus be avoided.

Characteristics within a family that determine subgroupings, alliances, and the formation of hostile camps have parallels in the family of man. Groupings within families can even be on an apparent "ethnic" basis, with some family members, for example, thinking of themselves as the northern Italian branch and others as the southern Italian branch. Erikson, as we have seen, speaks of ethnic units as pseudo-species (Erikson, 1966) and expresses the hope that they will eventually disappear. I have been impressed, however, by the fact that in the same circles in which nationalism was almost a dirty word about fifty years ago and there was enthusiasm for the ideas of world government and the international language Esperanto, there is now an acceptance of nationalism. To be sure, it is tempered by condemnation of chauvinism, and "separate but equal" is the avowed credo, but we have learned in racial relations that "separate but equal" is a polite cover for discrimination.

Examination of such changing waves of historical fashions in ego ideals has been a part of the work of the Committee on International Relations of the Group for the Advancement of Psychiatry. A GAP report on *Us and Them: The Psychology of Ethno-Nationalism* (1987) draws on some of the concepts that I have developed about multiple realities, particularly the notions related to primitivization of perception. The "narcissism of small differences" is evident when there is violent strife of closely related groups. To the outsider the difference in beliefs, life-style, even clothing between neighboring tribes may hardly be noticeable. But in the heat of battle the difference in clothing of the enemy tribesman, even if objectively minimal, looms large and is swollen with symbolic significance. Upon closer examination, one can see that primitivization of perceptual process in periods of stress leads to large intrapsychic differences, when completion of perceptual acts, the assessment of the difference in peacetime, would have led to the recognition of the smallness of the difference. Finally, and here I am returning to my basic themes, the differences move from the inner-psychological-temporal-animate to the outer-reified-spatial-inanimate when individual and cultural developments and transitions occur at times of great perceived danger. The extreme situation that may develop is the enemy's loss of the last remnants of recognizable human or even animate qualities. He can be treated and disposed of like so much wood, stone, or dirt.

Chapter 7

Psychoanalysis and Multiple Reality: Compatibility, Clinical Practice, and Prospects

In this concluding chapter, I will move back and forth between clinical and theoretical material, as I have done throughout this book. I will here venture further into theory, however, and I will also include speculations informed by developments in other fields. Partial summaries of ideas presented thus far will be embedded in an examination of their fit with psychoanalytic theory and also in tentative programmatic propositions about how they could be utilized in actual and in "thought" experiments.

In effect, I will be recapitulating the ontogeny of my own perceptions of human behavior, of psychoanalysis, and of relevant ideas and data from such fields as philosophy, epistemology, physics, and neurobiology. As with all such recapitulations, any designation of crisp boundaries between categories tends to distort the cumulative effect of the overlapping areas and their influences on one another. My aim here, which is an outgrowth of my experience in the consulting room and clinic, is to achieve a greater tolerance of ambiguity. In abandoning again and again the comfort of sharp outlines, we can paradoxically find our way to new, more comprehensive, and more precise epistemological, diagnostic, and therapeutic formulations.

The multiple-reality scheme developed here is related to the

term *state-specific learning*, which is encountered in contemporary psychiatric literature and had its antecedent in Federn's term
ego states (1952). Both terms refer to different organizations of
mental functioning, organizations that are relatively separate from
each other. My conceptualization of multiple realities adds two
features to these formulations: (1) it defines dimensions or parameters of the reality organizations, and (2) it specifies an ongoing
perceptual process of recapitulation of reality organizations. Together, these features have interacting clinical and theoretical consequences.

Let us first look at the clinical side. Psychoanalysis is not a
brief encounter, and in an enduring therapeutic encounter the
limitations, perhaps the falsifications, inherent in some diagnostic
classifications become apparent. Over an extended period, each
patient seems to have many different "disorders." This observation is not an appeal for the elimination of diagnoses, nor is it
simply an appeal to preserve the individual behind the diagnostic
category. After all, that would be only a repetition of a universal
but usually unheeded cry in this technological age of medicine. In
the context of the fluidity of multiple-reality organizations, the
structure of diagnostic thinking itself can be somewhat different.
The tolerance of such fluidity is at the center of this kind of
diagnostic thinking, and it is matched by the extent to which
tolerance of fluidity can be modified and increased in treatment;
perhaps better, flexible diagnostic thinking centers on the degree to
which obstacles to the creative expansion of the patient's tolerance
of ambiguity can be removed by appropriate treatment. Concern
with the tolerance for change is not very different from concern
with "ego strength" or with the "flexibility of the ego," but I have
specified some of the dimensions of the multiple-reality organizations in which such an ego must be able to move flexibly.

In the introduction to this book I observed how fashionable it is
now to have specialized clinics—depression clinics, premenstrual
tension clinics, phobia clinics—as well as specialized, or should I
say compartmentalized, treatment facilities for borderline and various psychotic disorders. The very fact that the term *borderline
disorder* has come into increasing use, however, may reflect discomfort with diagnostic boundaries that are too rigidly drawn. One

could argue that the diagnosis of "borderline" owes some of its relative longevity to its different meanings for different people. For Harold Searles, for instance, it means a syndrome at the border of psychotic and neurotic diagnoses. For others, in particular Otto Kernberg, it indicates a unique symptom constellation and especially the predominance of a specific level of defenses. Still others place borderline diagnoses primarily at the boundary between affective and cognitive disorders. The range of opinions is illustrated by the contributions of twenty-eight authors to *Borderline Personality Disorders*, edited by Peter Hartocollis (1977), which I have critically reviewed (Kafka, 1981).

My discussion of borderline disorders in chapter 4 illustrated how formulations that take multiple realities into account influence diagnostic and therapeutic thinking. For example, particular countertransference tensions are characteristic in work with patients whom the therapist is inclined to diagnose as "borderline." Because for much of the time these patients seem to share everyday reality organization with the therapist and seem to understand and to function in familiar frameworks, their peculiarities, their often infuriating actions and expectations, again and again surprise the therapist. My analysis of such "peculiarities" led to the discovery that the animate-inanimate confusion was particularly prominent for these patients. Recognition that this dimension of the multiple-reality scheme seemed to be in the foreground for them influenced my countertransference reactions and therefore ultimately my technical approach to them. Recognition of this kind helps diminish the confrontational element in the "clarifications" offered by the analytic therapist and influences the timing of interpretations. If it is possible to observe, for example, that the patient's ability to discriminate between animate and inanimate degenerates— becomes more primitive—when he or she is reacting to a particular conflict, then the analyst can shape resultant interpretations in the interests of enhancing the growth and development of such discrimination.

I recognize that my emphasis here on the animate-inanimate dichotomy might lead some analysts, notably Kernberg, to say that I am speaking of narcissistic rather than of borderline patients. In my experience, however, this narcissistic feature is characteristic of borderline patients and is diagnostically central, and I will discuss the issue in some detail later in the chapter. For my immediate purposes, however, it is not crucial whether narcissistic or borderline features of the patients are emphasized, since I wish primarily to illustrate some applications of the multiple-reality scheme and to show how such applications interdigitate with currently accepted psychoanalytic approaches.

The separateness of, the "unbridgeability" between, Federn's ego states and the conditions in which different state-specific learning occurs does have clinical consequences. As I pointed out in chapter 5, Federn believed, for instance, that different therapists should work with the same patient at times when he is flagrantly psychotic and when he is in remission. According to Federn, the therapist who is in contact with the patient during the psychotic period is contaminated by it and by its horror, and another therapist would be better for the "mental hygiene" approach that is appropriate for the patient in remission. Although I agree that there are deeply regressed conditions to which it may be impossible to find bridges during remissions, I have found that one of the essential functions of the therapist of psychotic patients is to enter their object world. He can do so only if he understands the nature of their object formation. As I elaborated earlier, the objects of the schizophrenic patient are understood as resulting from idiosyncratic subjective equivalences, which in turn are the result of a mix of perceptual acts at different stages of completion. Here, too, the multiple-reality scheme has specific clinical applications.

At this juncture we are approaching an area in which the merging of clinical and theoretical issues is particularly complex. I have sought to demonstrate that psychoanalysts do encounter the dimensions of my multiple-reality scheme in clinical work with neurotic patients—for instance, the animate-inanimate issue emerged for Mrs. A who suddenly and transiently experienced her husband as dead, "like a piece of wood." I believe that the moments in which these issues are encountered in the psychoanalytic treatment of neurotic patients are crucial and are related to structural change. Nevertheless, in the treatment of neurotic patients these structural reality issues are in the background most of the time, and the clinical focus is on the usual conflicts, defensive constellations, and transference issues familiar to the psychoanalytic clinician. It is usually only in retrospect that one recognizes the significance of crucial moments such as these I have been emphasizing. The analyst's awareness of such matters, however, may sensitize him to and keep him from neglecting the emergence of pertinent countertransference feelings.

In contrast, in work with some borderline patients and especially in the treatment of schizophrenic patients, the therapist's understanding of these structural reality issues must be in the therapeutic foreground. Here the analysis of the patient's object formation is essential, and this understanding permits the therapist to enter into and become established in the patient's object world.

What is the situation when a therapist has contact with a patient for a truly prolonged period and realizes that the "cross-sectional" diagnoses would be markedly different at various times during the patient's life? My own longest contact with a patient has extended over three decades. The only subgroup of schizophrenic diagnoses that nobody ever applied to her was "hebephrenic," and the range of nonpsychotic diagnoses that could have been applied by a clinician not familiar with her history was very wide. Here I want to emphasize that during periods of remission my work with her could hardly have been differentiated from psychoanalytic therapy with a neurotic patient; during one long period, if one had looked at that segment of the treatment without reference to other segments, the conflicts, the oedipal problems, and the transference configurations observed would have made differentiation from classical psychoanalysis difficult indeed.

I have come to believe that some of our difficulties in functioning as analytic therapists during some periods of work with such patients may be the result of the self-fulfilling prophecy that disaster will strike if we are more "analytic." To the degree to which the analytic therapist has become comfortable with his functioning in what can be considered multiple therapeutic realities, at least some patients can profit by his multiple functioning. Our caution may well be the result of mistakes early in the history of our field, when some psychoanalysts attempted unmodified psychoanalysis with patients whose psychosis was only thinly covered. This could indeed have extremely serious consequences. But the situation is different if the therapist is cognizant of the depth of the disturbance and follows the patient's lead during prolonged treatment if and when the patient indicates his or her wish, need, readiness for, and ability to handle exploratory psychoanalytic work.

It may be of interest to reflect on the number of different symptom-oriented clinics to which my long-standing patient could have been sent during this thirty-year period. She would certainly have qualified for clinics specializing in anxiety, phobias and panic, depression, and eating disorders in periods during which she was not particularly eager to talk about her hospitalizations. Of course, the pros and cons of symptom-oriented treatment must be considered in the context of the economics of therapy. Similarly, it is often pointed out that the battle between the champions of the psychiatric revolution that took patients from the attic and put them in institutions and the champions of the subsequent revolution that took them from the institutions and put them on the streets has not yet been decided. Obviously, the economic arguments, which must consider both direct and indirect costs, are complex ("Schizophrenia Costs. . . ," 1986). I want to emphasize here only one point frequently discussed in this context. On the basis of research findings, some psychiatrists recommend that families of chronic schizophrenic patients should be taught to dampen the expression of affect in order to reduce the frequency of relapse and rehospitalization. Others argue that the cost to the family of such an effort is too great. I would go beyond that and offer the observation that it was precisely the fear of expression of affect, which was thought to be catastrophic or literally deadly to an individual or a relationship, that worsened the tensions within the families of a number of my schizophrenic patients. The pathogenic consequences of the unspeakable have been widely documented, and I am here urging that the usefulness of analytic exploration of both individual and family conflicts not be overlooked in the rush toward cost-effective techniques of dealing with severe mental illness.

When we shift from clinical problems to theory, the most difficult aspect of the multiple-reality approach results from the formulation that the time-space dichotomy is one that itself is a developmental and therefore "temporal" step or achievement.

The ongoing perceptual recapitulation of the developmental sequence further complicates the picture, and the time-space dichotomy is thus multiply imbedded in time. As the discussion in chapter 3 has shown, we are here far from common sense.

We are, of course, also a long way from common sense in Longuet-Higgins's model of the central nervous system as a temporal hologram, a "holophone," in which each point in time has information about all other points in time. This is a model, however, that has profound psychological meaning. At each point in time we know something about our present, about our past, and about our projected future, which in turn influences our perception of the present and of the past. I cannot do justice here to the series of highly technical papers that Longuet-Higgins has written (1968, 1969, 1970), but certain questions that he raises will illustrate the pertinence of his work to these concerns. He postulates cells in the cerebral cortex that respond specifically to particular rhythms, just as there are known to be cells that fire only in the presence of specific visible features and arrays of cells that when briefly stimulated discharge rhythmically for some time afterward. He asks whether their thresholds for rhythmic firing can be altered by rhythmic stimulation.

The relevance of such work to my ideas about déjà vu phenomena, for instance, is readily apparent. I have been able to integrate Longuet-Higgins's work with my ideas in combination with Marian Kafka's findings that neurotransmitter receptors have different circadian rhythms altered differentially by psychoactive drugs (M. S. Kafka et al., 1983) and that there are hierarchies of rhythms in neurotransmitter receptors. We have summarized these ideas together with some of the multiple-reality formulations as follows:

> The model of a temporal hologram permits the non-local storage of memory. In the brain fast rhythms include neuronal firing and refractory period; slow rhythms, circadian rhythms. That neurotransmitter receptors have different circadian rhythms altered differentially by psychoactive drugs [and newer findings not involving drugs] supports the idea that rhythmic neuronal events are arranged in hierarchical levels of integration. Object constancies are derived from the subjective equivalence of stimulation patterns which are similar but not identical. Perceptual

acts may recapitulate their ontogeny. Stability of equivalence patterns depends on consistency in completing perceptual acts. Disordered temporal relationships of neuronal rhythms, by inconsistently interfering with perceptual act completion, can disrupt equivalence patterns and lead to thought disorder. As depressively tinged affect seems to determine the selection of stimulus-poor reference intervals, only part of the non-local storage bank may be addressed in some depressive disorders with diminished rather than disordered functioning. (Kafka and Kafka, 1983, p. 302)

In this summary, "selection of stimulus-poor reference intervals" refers to the experiment described in chapter 1 (Kafka, 1957a), in which individuals were found to select one out of a series of intervals as a baseline experience with which other experienced durations were then compared. The findings suggested that depressed affect was associated with the selection of the stimulus-poor reference intervals. In the introduction to this book I anticipated the criticism that I was dealing too much with cognition and not enough with affect. I also presented the argument that the affect-cognition dichotomy was not tenable, since drive-state, and therefore affect, determined the scanning activities that underlie perceptual and cognitive processes. But in connection with depressive affect I am now talking about diminished functioning—less or slower scanning apparently related to a state of diminished drive. This raises the theoretical question of the compatibility of these ideas with psychoanalytic formulations of depression.

In connection with my discussion of schizophrenic thought disorder in chapter 5, I remarked that one may have detailed and rather precisely worked out ideas about one aspect of a model and only crude and tentative formulations about other aspects of it. Intuitively, we are inclined to relate affect more directly than cognition to time—the rush of pleasant *ex*citement, the immobility related to the *depth* of depression, or, contrastingly, agitated depression, quiet elation, and other complexities of the phenomenology of time experience explored in earlier chapters.

By itself the notion of diminished expression of drive in depressive affect and depressive illness is not very informative. Consider, however, the following quote from a recent article by Leo Stone, in which he relates rich and differentiated clinical experience to a thorough discussion of early and evolving psychoanalytic theories: "This [depressive illness] is the simple and inclusive term in which one may subsume all those instances in which spontaneous primary affects are *hindered* in their expectable trend toward spontaneous subsidence or toward modification by *affirmative action*" (1986, p. 337; italics mine). Much, if not all, of Stone's paper could be read as a search for the dynamic reasons behind this "hindrance," this inhibition, or perhaps this slowing.[1] His discussion deals with object loss, the fate of narcissistic and anaclitic objects, aggression, conflict, orality, guilt, and much more. Although Stone is always the first to note how the coloring of the individual case transcends limited formulations, the connection of technical vocabulary to clinical data is particularly clear in his presentation. The *hindrance of affirmative action* is, in a sense, a phenomenological description of a central feature of depressive illness, but this is phenomenology intimately related to the genetics, dynamics, and economics of psychic life. My claim is that the phenomenology of perception has equally intimate connections to these determinants of mental functioning. Although I have elaborated the clinical usefulness of understanding these connections, let us look again at the relevant experimental data cited in chapter 5 and at the theoretical possibilities on the horizon.

Smith and Danielsson (1982) and Westerlundh and Smith (1983) have demonstrated that the defensive operations elucidated by psychoanalytic theory are essential for the understanding of findings of their experiments on perception. In other words, our familiar defenses operate in the microscopic time frame to which tachistoscopic perceptual experiments permit access. "Masking"

---

1. Stone is concerned with unconscious inhibition, unconscious slowing, in depressed patients. A conscious and deliberate defensive manipulation of time can be observed in some patients who are not primarily depressed. Although some such manipulation is common, in my experience it has been of central clinical importance in patients who have suffered from actual early parental physical assaults or who have witnessed such assaults and sought to protect themselves by becoming immobile and "blending into the wall." Inactivity or postponed reactivity after unpleasant experience of thoughts—until, after several days, the perception has faded—may characterize such patients. They may also find it hard to understand why others come so rapidly to conclusions about them. These patients may "hide their light under a bushel" and feel misunderstood, chronically underestimated, because others do not wait until the light is exposed.

is also a technique used in a number of tachistoscopic perceptual experiments. These findings and the pertinent literature are summarized by Holzman (1987). Essentially this technique involves the presentation of at least two different stimuli in succession. By varying the parameters of the various exposures, one can determine the differences in the timing of the second exposure that affect interference or noninterference in the "perception" of the first stimulus. Schizophrenic patients need a greater interval between the two stimuli than control subjects do in order to perceive the first stimulus without interference from the second.

Such a finding is consonant with my clinically derived hypothesis about differences in perceptual processing in schizophrenic patients. Among the parameters that can be varied in such masking experiments, of course, are not only intervals between stimuli and the duration of the stimulus exposure but also the content of the stimulus. The design of the content could variously present not only such "determinants" (as in Rorschach tests) as color and human, animal, or "inanimate" movement but also specific representational scenes (like those in thematic apperception tests) and even individually designed scenes that take into account the individual's development and the development of his defenses. Numerous other experimental possibilities offer opportunities to explore these hypotheses—for example, devices that register eye movement, which permit us to study tracking. The effect of paranoid vigilance on perceptual style could be compared, for instance, to the effect of a hysterical defensive constellation. The combined possibilities of brain visualization techniques, such as PET-scan and magnetic resonance, might permit the localization of cerebral activities when, for instance, specific perceptual processes or *perceptual defenses* are operative. Opportunities for using, confirming, modifying, or extending psychoanalytic theory in the context of sophisticated studies of perception are likely to expand. Clinicians disagree about the relevance of developments in theoretical understanding for psychoanalytic therapeutic technique generally, and it is an open question whether psychoanalytic understanding of perceptual processes in depressed patients will directly influence therapeutic technique with some of them. For me, however, theoretical exploration not only has added a richer background for the clinical work but also has influenced it in subtle ways, even when the immediate connection cannot be so clearly demonstrated as in the case of schizophrenic object formation. The analyst's alertness to previously neglected dimensions, I believe, can permit more correctly attuned responses.

Longuet-Higgins's model of temporally or rhythmically addressable memory is also compatible with the spatial localizations that are becoming more possible through new visualization techniques. But for the moment I would like to turn to some interesting speculations that his model permits concerning the size of organisms, the inner-outer question. Speaking of memories that can be addressed temporally rather than spatially, he evokes the image of banks of oscillators with resonant frequencies and damping constants: "They will behave rather like the strings of a piano, which will be set into oscillation by singing into the piano with the sustaining pedal held down. In this case the air acts as both input and output channel, and one hears afterwards the combined effect of the individual oscillations" (1968, p. 329). Admittedly I am approaching his technical work with considerable poetic license, but his reference to the air acting as both input and output channel brings to mind, for instance, Loewald's discussion of the mother-infant unit, where objects are located, in a manner of speaking, between the two. Arnold Modell's work in *Object Love and Reality* (1968) is also evoked rather vividly. In studying the early cave paintings, he found that prehistoric artists used three-dimensional characteristics of the cave walls, characteristics that suggested the forms of specific animals, as structural parts of their paintings. The object is, so to speak, between whatever created the wall and the creator of the painting. Extending even further the exploration of the question of the size of the organism, who or what does the remembering when the remembering unit is not fixed but changes its size and temporal configuration? The difficulties discussed in chapter 3, related to our attachment to common sense, never quite leave us.

Since techniques for visualization of the locus of cerebral activities are becoming ever more sophisticated and a model for temporal addressability of memories exists, it is possible that we will be able to localize *spatially* brain regions in which different *rhythms* prevail. There are many opportunities here for research efforts that would integrate local brain visualization, data about differential neurotransmitter activities and rhythms (M. S. Kafka et al., 1986a, 1986b, 1986c), clinical data about phase delays in depression, and psychoanalytically informed behavioral and perceptual studies. I would like, however, to move now from these practicable biological laboratory studies into more speculative territory and consider the whole area of thought experiments that include consideration of spatial and temporal "structures." In doing so, I want to reemphasize the possible connections between structural change in the psychoanalytic sense and the differences between animate and inanimate structures. Sequences that are possible in temporal structures are also profoundly connected with questions of causality and thus with meaning.

Before going further, let me recapitulate some of the more theoretical issues with which I have been dealing. The more philosophical polarity of my preoccupation with time is related to the zeitgeist derived from modern physics. Commonsense matter has disappeared. Even biology deals with systems of energy—for instance, when molecular biologists discuss the very nature of cell membranes. Let us recall Longuet-Higgins's temporal model of the brain and the observation that the focus on time permits a new perspective on the mind-body problem and fits in with Loewald's radical characterization of time as the inner fiber of mind.

The advantages of clinical attention to the temporal are manifold. The link between clinical and theoretical issues is underlined again when we consider that the meaning of a situation depends on when the situation is perceived as beginning and ending. Attention to idiosyncratic temporal organization and disorganization enlarges the repertoire of possible meanings with which the patient can be heard or observed. The extension of the idea of subjective equivalence to the temporal dimension opens new clinical and theoretical vistas. Although the term *subjectively equivalent stimuli* refers to the content of perception, the concept of subjective equivalence can also be applied to formal temporal characteristics. We know that intervals of different "objective" duration may be perceived as being of equal duration and that "objectively" equal intervals may be perceived subjectively as very different from each other. We do have some information about factors that influence such temporal "distortions." Once again, the need to understand the functioning of affects enters my exposition, which at first seems cognitively oriented. Ever-changing patterns of distortions, patterns of patterns, determine the perceptual temporal texture of our contact with the 'outer and the inner world. Which "constancies" are maintained, and the very meaning of "constancy," in a world that one approaches with acute temporal awareness are questions that acquire a new depth. My focus on time, however, leads us still further and again into an area where clinic and theory meet.

Psychoanalytic listening is informed by attention to contiguity. The psychoanalyst, by using free-floating (I prefer the term *hovering*) attention, tries also to free himself from that which contiguity sometimes seems intent on imposing. The psychoanalyst, so to speak, continuously changes temporal lenses, which range all the way from zoom to wide angle. He even tries to utilize several lenses at once. Why? First, because he knows that defensive operations—that is, defenses against the emergence into awareness of meanings and affects—utilize temporal tools, temporal disconnections, and false connections. The psychoanalyst, and to some extent every dynamic therapist, must therefore be capable of assuming, with correct "timing," a wider temporal stance than the patient. A widening of the patient's stance is an implicit analytic goal because the very notion of change, of changing awareness, of insight, implies both the development of a sense of connection between matters that previously seemed unconnected and the abandonment of false connections. For example, a patient might be helped to recognize the connection between his sense of guilt and the death of his brother. At the same time the patient can be helped to realize that his baby brother did not die simply because he may have once wished him dead. The discovery of meaning in what had once seemed haphazard and the discovery of the falsity of apparent connections (in a sense, the rediscovery of the haphazard) are essential ingredients of the psychoanalytic venture.

Beyond that, however, the very "meaning of meaning" is deeply rooted in the temporal dimension. Since psychoanalysis has taught us the operations, as it were, through which meaning is discovered and dissolved, since it has opened the door to unconscious meaning, this very expansion of our consciousness and of our self-consciousness regarding our operations has also underlined the question of whether we *ever* go far enough in our connecting, reconnecting, and dissolving of connections. Could it be that the universe is meaningless and chaotic and owes all its apparent causality, order, and meaning to the projection of our needs for those characteristics?[2] In chapter 4 I discussed an experiment (Bavelas, 1970) demonstrating the persistence of erroneous convictions regarding causality, the tenacity with which people refuse to accept randomness of events. The tenacity of such refusal is central in Jacques Monod's thesis (1972) that we live in a chaotic universe upon which we project, impose a false order, that we create, construct, a false causality and attempt to deny essential randomness and chaos.

This is a philosophical issue which we encounter in the laboratories of psychoanalysis and psychopathology, where chaos and disorder can become manifest especially when the belief in one causal connection has been loosened and before another set of beliefs has taken root, when one way of understanding the meaning of the sequence of one's life events is about to give way to another interpretation. New convictions are reached, but the very experience of profound change, the shattering of deeply held convictions when aspects of our development are relived and reinterpreted in the heat of psychoanalytic transference, also underlines at least the theoretical ultimate uncertainty of our convictions. The new experience is how much a new conviction can coexist with a profound knowledge that convictions can change. Shortly before termination of his treatment, a patient summarized such experiences: "Psychoanalysis is getting out of dead ends."

Order and structure are topics in which clinical and philosophical preoccupations meet. As I commented earlier, in clinical psychoanalysis we encounter the word *structure* in the context of structural change. The study of change in psychoanalysis and an examination of the concept of structure in that context have led

2. I will not consider here theological arguments that address the meaning of such needs and essentially draw the conclusion that the very existence of the need is proof of the existence of something that corresponds to it.

discovered and dissolved, since it has opened the door to uncon-facet of the multiple-reality theme I have been describing as the animate and the inanimate object. It is a frequent clinical observa-tion that presenting complaints become less significant as the treatment progresses. Sometimes this may be so because a com-plaint or a symptom was only the "official," acceptable reason for entering treatment, while other and deeper reasons were close to awareness from the beginning. A shift in the areas in which the "live action" is in treatment, a shift in the themes that are "ani-mated" and those that are "deadly" and uninteresting, may per-haps be traced to the early differentiation between the animate and the inanimate—that is, there may be a connection between struc-tural change in the psychoanalytic sense, the shift from insight to active change, and the early distinction between the animate and inanimate worlds. I am here speaking of inanimate objects as those that either do not react to our actions or at least react differently from those that are "alive." The topic of how the reaction to death may or may not be related specifically to the infant's developing ability to distinguish the animate from the inanimate may also be pertinent here.

Here again the clinical material that I have encountered in my experience and infant research data remind me of more philosophi-cal themes concerning the structure of the animate and the inani-mate. I think of Henri Bergson's description of the stone as being different from animate matter because it has only one (unchang-ing) perception of the universe, which again raises the topic of time. Perception involves making contact with, dealing with, a contrast or at least a difference—hence a temporal movement to and fro. By referring to the stone's unchanging perception, by using a term ordinarily limited to what animate beings can do, by using the term at the absurd limit, Bergson points to the funda-mental temporal distinction between the animate and inanimate realms. As I said earlier, Sartre's distinction between "process" and "praxis" deals with the difference between events that result from inanimate occurrences (a thunderstorm, for instance) and those resulting from animate action, be it consciously or uncon-sciously intended by an animate being.

On this most theoretical level, the nature of this particular structural difference has also led me to the fascinating work of the physicist Ilya Prigogine (1976). He has shown how under certain conditions "new" structures can be formed in physical systems. With extreme differences in temperature in different parts of a liquid, temperature distribution shifts from diffusion to the formation of hexagonal currents. Prigogine believes that his findings are pertinent to the formation of new structures in biological and social systems. Perhaps there is a bridge here to our understanding of animate and inanimate structures and at least a distant connection to the clinically observed switching, the animation and deanimation, that I have discussed.

Among other switching phenomena that have received much attention recently in psychiatric literature, the biology of manic-depressive mood switches in a major focus of interest. The German word *überschnappen* is also relevant here, referring to sudden shifts in mental functioning in a broad sense to becoming crazy or disorganized; it focuses perhaps more on thought disorder, although it does not exclude affective change. In such phenomena, it is usually the analogy between sudden changes in the physical system and sudden changes in the clinical picture that has captured the attention of psychiatrists. Arnold Mandell et al. (1982) speculate that the switches psychiatrists observe may be related to actual shifts in the mode of neuronal transmission. Mandell believes that cellular transmission—that is, neuron to neuron—may under certain circumstances be replaced by a mode of transmission in which the brain, or part of it, suddenly functions as the semiliquid mass that also characterizes its physical reality. If such a view were to receive support from empirical findings, the multiple-reality theme would be anchored in data that were beyond my horizon when I formulated my ideas. Could such switches be connected with shifts from spatial localization to temporal addressability, to my ideas connecting experiential multiple realities, including shifts in the animate-inanimate experience, to different temporal, different rhythmic organizations of the brain?

There is also a palpable connection between the animate-inanimate dichotomy and affective life. The idea of being animate corresponds to the experience of oneself as an autonomous center for the initiation of action. There is an obvious connection to changes in mood, since mood changes are intimately related to shifts in the experience of oneself as powerful or helpless. One patient's high moods were related to identification with a flamboyant father—for example, as a child she had sat on her father's lap and "controlled" a small airplane that he was piloting, even flying upside down, no less. Her low moods were related to falls from grace and experiences of impuissance in the family. Recovery of memories and reconstruction of this material in a long analysis with intense transference developments proved therapeutically effective. This patient's clinical picture descriptively had been indistinguishable from that of patients who are now routinely diagnosed as having an affective disorder and treated with lithium (as my patient had been prior to my work with her) or antidepressant drugs. I believe that in such patients therapeutic approaches may benefit from the simple and explicit recognition of a possible link between the animate-inanimate axis and the polarity of a sense of power (or power over something) and its affective component, on the one hand, and impuissance and its affective component, on the other hand. The wall that had separated the markedly hypomanic and severely depressed states of my patient with the flamboyant father was a high one indeed. Perhaps different degrees of animation characterize different states—analogous to conditions of state-specific learning and Federn's different ego states.

Let us turn now to an examination of related issues in some borderline and narcissistic patients. Such patients do not differentiate between Sartre's praxis and process, the results of animate volition and of the forces of nature. They force the analytic therapist to deal with this theme when they act as if they were "entitled" to be treated by the forces of nature in a special and individualized fashion. The forces of nature are not "entitled" to be inanimate.

The term *entitlement* is associated with the concept of narcissism, and my reference to borderline patients in this context is not accidental. In Kernberg's schema, narcissistic disorders are a subgroup of the borderline personality disorders. I believe, however, that splitting defenses have such a prominent place in his understanding of the borderline disorders and at the same time are so central in his conceptualization of the narcissistic disorders that his subgrouping runs into some conceptual difficulty. To what extent can the features of "ego weakness" that for Kernberg characterize the borderline disorder be understood—rather than merely described—without reference to the splitting mechanisms that are also the central feature of narcissism? I mention these details of theory here because the idea that ego weakness may have something to do with early difficulties in establishing and maintaining the boundary between the animate and the inanimate is compatible with my approach to these problems.

In the early psychoanalytic literature, narcissistic disorders referred to the psychoses because it was believed that there was a deficiency of (external) object cathexes and an oversupply of narcissistic cathexes. Federn, whose work is now unjustly neglected, saw in psychosis a deficiency of cathexes at the boundary of the ego. In this formulation the psychotic individual was thus unable to discern whether a stimulus had penetrated from the outside or had an internal origin. Hallucinations, for instance, could not be differentiated from perceptions of the "real" world. There is an affinity between this early psychoanalytic formulation and my idea that a lack of the ability to establish or maintain the animate-inanimate boundary—or at least a weakness in it—represents a major issue in psychopathology.

The diagnostic significance of this issue is a complex one, and I emphatically do not want to link all problems of animate-inanimate differentiation with a diagnosis of psychosis. As I hope has been clear from my text, I consider the ability to treat the same object as animate on some occasions and inanimate on others and in other contexts as an essential component of the adaptive and creative use of multiple realities. Nevertheless, a somewhat unexpected bridge may be discovered between the older psychoanalytic uses of the term *narcissistic disorder* and the more current uses of the term if we consider that animate-inanimate boundary difficulties and ways of handling these difficulties characterize both the old and the new diagnostic categories.

The ability to treat the same object as both animate and inanimate is a characteristic that is often discussed in a developmental framework and is related to Winnicott's work on transitional objects. The connections between Winnicott's ideas and mine have been documented in chapters 2 and 4, in studying how a patient may use his or her own body as a transitional object and in the study of rituals. My emphasis on the creative and therapeutic uses of a multiple reality that encompasses the realities of the same object as both animate and inanimate obviously also has considerable affinity with Winnicott's ideas; he emphasizes the creative and therapeutic uses of an object that during particular developmental and usefully regressive moments is neither animate nor inanimate but is both simultaneously, or "transitional" between the two.

My extension or elaboration of the transitional realm goes beyond Winnicott's formulation when I introduce the idea of the transitional between the spatial (or "material") and the temporal, since the spatial is also associated with the inanimate realm and the temporal with the animate one. Gabel's (1967) understanding of ideology as a nonpsychological, spatial, and reified structure that can be contrasted with the temporal characteristics of mental life has led him to consider the similarities between political ideologies and the mind of the schizophrenic patient. In discussing rituals, I have similarly considered mental deposits of the past—and thus perhaps ideologies—as connected with psychopathology, stagnation, and the ritualistic rather than with the genuine ritual, in which transitional experiences can be recapitulated and the connection to root experiences reaffirmed. The ritual object is at the same time the unique, most concrete, specific inanimate material entity and the most condensed symbol of the animus, the spirit, the alive and abstract intentionality of the group, tribe, or ethnic or religious assembly. In contrast, I have emphasized the pathology of the "single reality," the reification and "spatialization" of the psyche. Accordingly, my therapeutic approach focuses on the mobilization associated with multiple realities.

The multiple realities I propose are organized along (1) a spatial-temporal axis, (2) a size-of-organism axis (theoretically, from cellular or even intracellular to the large social unit, but more immediately or practically, from individual to family or group), and (3) an inanimate-animate axis. Certain correspondences, relationships, and perhaps equations exist between the ever-changing positions on the axes of my multiple-reality scheme. As I have stressed throughout this book, more spatial corresponds to more inanimate or reified, and more temporal to more animate, more mental or psychological. The issue of the size of the organism seems to be anchored in a reified spatial dimension, but the person who sees himself as part of the group also at that moment changes his temporal perspective since the unit that determines his "reality" may well extend beyond his individual life span.

The reference to the term *equation* in the paragraph above needs further elaboration. It is an ambitious term, but I believe it is justified because it deals, after all, with the relationship of the material, the spatial, with time. One equation that has changed our world is Einstein's $e=mc^2$. The consideration of developments in modern physics when we discuss problems in our field is not new. Marie Bonaparte (1940) informs us that the problem did not escape Freud when he considered the timelessness of the unconscious and that he was well aware of what I would call the multiple realities of wave and particle theories. It seems to me that the term *multiple realities* applies when the physicists tell us that certain phenomena can be conceptualized or understood only in the framework of particle theory, whereas others can be managed only in the framework of wave theory. The dichotomy we encounter between the static-reified-spatial-inanimate and the fluid-temporal-animate seems to relate to particle and wave. Despite warnings I mentioned early in this book against facile philosophizing or psychologizing of insights derived from modern physics, perhaps some considerations derived from that discipline can inform psychological perspectives on multiple realities, even though the data that demand such perspectives come from the consulting room. Einstein's equation establishes a relationship between energy, mass, and the square of the speed of light—that is, time. An equation points out that factors do not "exist" in isolation but have a potential for transformation or translation; this phenomenon is not totally removed from the shifts we encounter clinically when a frozen, reified position, a rigid stance, becomes animated or reanimated, becomes fluid, temporal, and psychologically alive. Thus, it is difficult not to think of the probable pertinence of the theory of relativity to the body-mind problem, and thus to our field, especially at a time when Eric Kandel has demonstrated physical structural changes on the cellular level that derive from the experience of the neuron (1983).

Once one decides to consider the world of modern physics as pertinent to work in our field, even wider vistas open up. The equation $e=mc^2$ has also been interpreted to mean that mass is frozen energy. Modern cosmology postulates an original energy cauldron, an "id" that lacks "structure" in the sense that molecules and atoms cannot exist in it. There is, in a sense, a lack of "objects." The expansion of the universe with the accompanying lowering of the temperature leads to the formation of mass, of atoms and molecules, of objects. Perhaps each perceptual act can be understood not only as recapitulating the ontogeny of perception but also as recapitulating the creation of the universe. The perceptual act is the creative expansion from (nonmass) energy to the formation of mass, of structure, of objects. Before I stop my excursion into cosmology, I want to cite an extreme example of the extent to which commonsense efforts to understand the world are being challenged. One serious attempt to help us understand notions of reversed entropy, for example, appeared recently in the daily press. A *Washington Post* article of December 26, 1986, about the physicist Stephen Hawking bore the headline: "Physicist Theorizes on Direction of Time." The idea that the psychological present is informed or formed by a two-directional temporal scheme, the future and the past, is perhaps somewhat less beyond conceptual reach at a moment in history when the reversible time issue hits the newspapers.

It is a somewhat less bold step to relate findings from computer science to aspects of our field. According to Michael Rabin (1977, 1987), the introduction of randomness paradoxically leads to greater order (and better decisions) when large numbers of computers work together on decision-making tasks. Perhaps this is relevant to my critique of the double-bind hypothesis and to the idea that it is the absence of tolerance for ambiguity, not the paradoxical communication pattern, that is likely to be pathogenic. I have described how I went from clinical material to Gödel's formal demonstration of the necessity for ambiguity. When I found that the double-bind theorists had ignored one major component of Russell's *De Principia Mathematica*, Gödel's name was not widely known outside the field of mathematics. Since then, Hofstadter, in his *Gödel, Escher, Bach* (1979), has made him an intellectual household word. As psychoanalytic students of the mind, do we need to understand more formal links between Rabin's and Gödel's work, which is central to students of artificial intelligence? Is it possible that the absolute absence of randomness leads to disorder, perhaps even to psychotic disorder?

In at least one sense, grandiose thoughts about the connection between the multiple-reality theme and expansive cosmological parallels are highly pertinent to clinical work. Although it has been said in many different ways that each individual is a universe and creates a universe, an effort to formulate a technical description of its creation, whatever the intrinsic merits or limitations of that description, fosters in the therapist a respect for the details of the individualized processes by which each patient forms both the more ephemeral and the more lasting aspects of his realities. Such added respect colors the atmosphere of the consulting room and underlines the analyst's nonjudgmental stance.

For the analyst, the work is always "in progress." Conceptualization of the patient's problems must always be unfinished as meanings and realities come and go, as connections move from haphazard to persuasive and vice versa. When the analyst finds that he is able to take a position, he recognizes at the same time that it is a contextual position and that it is in response to a change in the patient's contextual position, both temporally and spatially.

Because of such fluctuations, development of the nonjudgmental stance is a truly major component of the psychoanalyst's training. The arguments that a value-free position is unreachable in practice have led some clinicians to downplay the importance of the effort to approximate it. The "moral" questions in psychoanalysis, the questions of intentionality and will (Smith, 1976), are also ultimately questions of "free" will and (psychic) determinism. In discussing this topic from the viewpoint of sociobiology, Wilson (1975) gives the example of the behavior of a bee that is being observed by a scientist who has information about its genetic makeup, its life history, and its environment. While the observing scientist can make accurate predictions about the bee's behavior, presumably the "experience" in the bee's "mind" is one of free-dom of choice. Although the cross-species component of the example complicates the picture, the freedom of choice question is reduced by Wilson—as it is in somewhat different ways by many authors—to an "inside-outside" question that is related to the question of the size of the organism. From outside it is "deter-mined" and from inside it is "free." My discussions of perceptual recapitulation in ontogenetic, phylogenetic, and even cosmologi-cal terms and of the ever-changing size of the organism being studied (and studying itself) also lead to a less absolute or fixed view of what is outside and what is inside; inside and outside can be understood to be either in constant flux or, if the temporal exten-sion of the discussion is kept in mind, to coexist. Transference-related transactions in psychoanalysis extend the range of the size-of-the-organism experience and thus lead the patient to expe-riences of autonomy, to possibilities of self-initiation beyond the preanalytic limitations.

    As I come to the end of my pendulum swings, moving from clinical data through clinical musing toward theorizing and then back to the epistemological thoughts originating in what I have called "the clinical laboratory of philosophy," I wonder how many familiar chords I have struck in the reader. Has my reader also experienced with regret the lack of bridges—or the lack of *recog-nition* of bridges—between philosophical and formal logical prop-ositions and psychoanalytic thought, a lack illustrated by the ab-sence of both "Freud" and "psychoanalysis" from the index of Hofstadter's *Gödel, Escher, Bach*? A clinical approach that reaches far enough must deal with the organization of the individ-ual's realities—a problem that can go beyond the patently clinical. Essentially no propositions dealing with the nature of reality are too formal if we are to remain profoundly and appropriately recep-tive to the patient's transitional formlessness when new structures are in the making.

    The field of psychoanalysis itself illustrates a context of multi-ple realities as it simultaneously moves in different directions that expand and enrich both clinical and academic viewpoints. At one extreme, Helmut Thomä and Horst Kächele's recent two-volume survey (1987) of psychoanalytic practice exemplifies sophisticated psychoanalytic scientific empiricism. At the other extreme, Janet Malcolm's description (1987) of current literary psychoanalytic extrapolations—many inspired by contemporary French analysts and philosophers and including transferential analyses of Freud's writings—is no less illuminating to both therapists and humanists. Students of human behavior who can accept such alternate approaches without feeling constrained to choose between them are finding that the mysteries of the resultant more complex world become less forbidding—and even inviting.

Have I struck familiar chords? Freud (1914) said that termination is near when the analysand (the reader?) feels that he has known it all along.

References

Abramson, H. A., ed. 1959. *The use of LSD in psychotherapy.* New York: Josiah Macy, Jr., Foundation.

Ackerman, N. W. 1963. Family diagnosis and therapy. In *Current psychiatric therapies*, vol. 3, edited by J. H. Masserman. New York: Grune & Stratton.

American Psychiatric Association. 1980. *Diagnostic and statistical manual of mental disorders (DSM-III).* 3d ed. Washington, D.C.: American Psychiatric Association.

Anderson, C. M. 1983. A psychoeducational model of family treatment for schizophrenia. In *Psychosocial intervention in schizophrenia*, edited by H. Stierlin, L. C. Wynne, and M. Wirsching. Berlin: Springer-Verlag.

Arieti, S. 1963. Studies of thought processes in contemporary psychiatry. *American Journal of Psychiatry* 120:58–64.

Arlow, J. 1959. The structure of the déjà vu experience. *Journal of the American Psychoanalytic Association* 7:611–31.

Artiss, K. L. 1962. *Milieu therapy and schizophrenia.* New York: Grune & Stratton.

Bakker, C. B., and Amini, F. B. 1961. Observations on the psychotomimetic effects of Sernyl. *Comprehensive Psychiatry* 2:269–80.

Bateson, G., Jackson, D. D., Haley, J., and Weakland, J. H. 1956. Toward a theory of schizophrenia. *Behavioral Science* 1:251–64.

Bavelas, A. 1970. Description of experiment on persistence of erroneous convictions regarding "causality." In *Problem-solving and*

search behavior under non-contingent rewards, edited by J. C.
Wright. Ann Arbor, Mich.: University Microfilms.

Berlyne, D. E. 1966. Conflict and arousal. *Scientific American*
215:82–87.

Bonaparte, M. 1940. Time and the unconscious. *International Journal of Psycho-Analysis* 21:427–68.

Borges, J. L. 1964. A new refutation of time. In *Labyrinths*, edited by
D. A. Yates and J. E. Irby. New York: New Directions.

Boring, E. G. 1933. *The physical dimensions of consciousness*. New
York: Century.

Bowen, M. 1961. The family as the unit of study and treatment.
American Journal of Orthopsychiatry 31:40–60.

Brody, W., and Hayden, M. 1957. Intra-team reactions: Their relation to the conflicts of the family in treatment. *American Journal of
Orthopsychiatry* 27:349–55.

Burnham, D. L. 1966. The special-problem patient: Victim or agent
of splitting? *Psychiatry* 29:105–22.

Eissler, K. 1953. The effect of the structure of the ego on psychoanalytic technique. *Journal of the American Psychoanalytic Association* 1:104–43.

Erikson, E. H. 1966. Ontogeny of ritualization. In *Psychoanalysis—
A general psychology: Essays in honor of Heinz Hartmann*, edited
by R. M. Loewenstein et al. New York: International Universities
Press.

Federn, P. 1952. *Ego psychology and the psychoses*. New York:
Basic Books.

Freud, S. 1913. *Totem and taboo*. In *Standard edition of the complete
psychological works*, vol. 13. London: Hogarth, 1955.

———. 1914. Fausse reconnaissance ("déjà raconté") in psychoanalytic treatment. In *Standard edition of the complete psychological works*, vol. 13. London: Hogarth, 1955.

———. 1915. The unconscious. In *Standard edition of the complete
psychological works*, vol. 14. London: Hogarth, 1955.

———. 1919. The "uncanny." In *Standard edition of the complete
psychological works*, vol. 17. London: Hogarth, 1955.

Fry, W. F., Jr. 1968. *Sweet madness: A study of humor*. Palo Alto,
Calif.: Pacific Books.

Gaarder, K. 1963. A conceptual model of schizophrenia. *AMA Archives of General Psychiatry* 8:590–98.

Gaarder, K., and Kafka, J. S. 1963. An experimental case study of the effects of Sernyl. Presented at Chestnut Lodge Symposium, Rockville, Maryland.

Gabel, J. 1962. *La fausse conscience: Essai sur la réification*. Paris: Les Editions de Minuit.

———. 1967. *Ideologie und Schizophrenie: Formen der Entfrendung*. Frankfurt am Main: S. Fischer Verlag.

Gödel, K. 1931. Über formal unentscheidbare Sätze der Principia Mathematica und verwandter Systeme: I. *Monatschrifte für Mathematik Physik* 38:173–98.

Goodrich, D. W., and Boomer, D. S. 1963. Experimental assessment of modes of conflict resolution. *Family Process* 2:15–24.

Graetz, H. 1893. *Geschichte der Juden*. Leipzig: Leiner & Löwit.

Green, A. 1977. The borderline concept. In *Borderline personality disorders*, edited by P. Hartocollis. New York: International Universities Press.

Green, H. 1964. *I never promised you a rose garden*. New York: Holt, Rinehart & Winston.

Greenspan, S. I. 1982. Three levels of learning: A developmental approach to "awareness" and mind-body relations. *Psychoanalytic Inquiry* 1:659–94.

Grotstein, J. S. 1977. The psychoanalytic concept of schizophrenia: I. The dilemma. II. Reconciliation. *International Journal of Psycho-Analysis* 58:403–52.

Group for the Advancement of Psychiatry. In press. *Us and them: The psychology of ethno-nationalism*. New York: Brunner/Mazel.

Gunderson, J. G., and Carroll, A. 1983. Clinical considerations from empirical research. In *Psychosocial intervention in schizophrenia*, edited by H. Stierlin, L. C. Wynne, and M. Wirsching. Berlin: Springer-Verlag.

Handke, P. 1969. *Die Innenwelt der Aussenwelt der Innenwelt*. Frankfurt am Main: Suhrkamp. Eng. trans. by Michael Roloff. New York: Continuum, 1974.

Hartmann, H. 1939. *Ego psychology and the problem of adaptation*. New York: International Universities Press, 1958.

Hartocollis, P., ed. 1977. *Borderline personality disorders: The concept, the syndrome, the patient*. New York: International Universities Press.

Hayman, A. 1969. What do we mean by "id"? *Journal of American Psychoanalytic Association* 17:353–80.

Hoch, R. H., Pennes, H. H., and Cattell, J. P. 1958. Psychoses produced by the administration of drugs. In *Chemical concepts of psychosis*, edited by M. Rinkel. New York: McDowell, Oblensky.

Hofstadter, D. R. 1979. *Gödel, Escher, Bach.* New York: Basic Books.

Hohage, R., and Kuebler, J. C. 1985. The emotional insight rating scale. Paper presented at Ulmer Werkstatt, University of Ulm.

Hollos, S., and Ferenczi, S. 1922. *Zur Psychoanalyse der paralytischen Geistesstörung.* Vienna: Internationaler Psychoanalytischer Verlag.

Holzman, P. 1987. Recent studies of psychophysiology in schizophrenia. *Schizophrenia Bulletin* 13:49–75.

Israeli, N. 1936. *Abnormal personality and time.* New York: Science Press.

Jaffe, D. S. 1971. The role of ego modification and the task of structural change in the analysis of a case of hysteria. *International Journal of Psycho-Analysis* 52:375–93.

Kafka, J. S. 1957a. A method for studying the organization of time experience. *American Journal of Psychiatry* 114:546–53.

———. 1957b. On the experience of duration in psychotherapy. Presented at Chestnut Lodge Symposium, Rockville, Maryland.

———. 1964. Technical applications of a concept of multiple reality. *International Journal of Psycho-Analysis* 45:575–78.

———. 1966. Practical and conceptual developments concerning work with families. Paper presented at Southern Divisional Meeting, American Psychiatric Association, Hollywood, Florida.

———. 1969. The body as transitional object: A psychoanalytic study of a self-mutilating patient. *British Journal of Medical Psychology* 42:207–12.

———. 1971a. A psychoanalytic perspective on the organization and integration of time experience. Paper presented at panel on the Experience of Time, American Psychoanalytic Association, December.

———. 1971b. Ambiguity for individuation: A critique and reformulation of double-bind theory. *Archives of General Psychiatry* 25:232–39.

———. 1972. The experience of time. Report on panel, American Psychoanalytic Association, December 1971. *Journal of the American Psychoanalytic Association* 20:650–67.

———. 1977. On reality: An examination of object constancy, ambiguity, paradox, and time. In *Thought, consciousness, and reality,* vol. 2 of *Psychiatry and the humanities*, edited by J. H. Smith. New Haven: Yale University Press.

———. 1981. Review of *Borderline personality disorders*, edited by P. Hartocollis. *Journal of the American Psychoanalytic Association* 29:236–47.

———. 1983. Challenge and confirmation in ritual action. *Psychiatry* 46:31–39.

Kafka, J. S., and Bolgar, H. 1949. Notes on the clinical use of future autobiographies. *Rorschach Research Exchange and Journal of Projective Techniques* 13:341–46.

Kafka, J. S., and Gaarder, K. 1964. Some effects of the therapist's LSD experience on his therapeutic work. *American Journal of Psychotherapy* 18:236–43.

Kafka, J. S., and Kafka, M. S. 1983. Timing process and mental illness. *Abstracts, Seventh World Congress of Psychiatry*. Vienna.

Kafka, J. S., and McDonald, J. W. 1965. The latent family in the intensive treatment of the hospitalized schizophrenic patient. *Current psychiatric therapies*, vol. 5, edited by J. S. Masserman. New York: Grune & Stratton.

Kafka, M. S., Benedito, M. A., Blendy, J. A., and Tokola, N. A. 1986a. Circadian rhythms in neurotransmitter receptors in discrete rat brain regions. *Chronobiology International* 3:91–100.

Kafka, M. S., Benedito, M. A., and Roth, R. H. 1986b. Circadian rhythms in catecholamine metabolites and cyclic nucleotide production. *Chronobiology International* 3:101–15.

Kafka, M. S., Benedito, M. A., Steele, L. K., et al. 1986c. Relationships between behavioral rhythms, plasma corticosterone and hypothalamic circadian rhythms. *Chronobiology International* 3:117–22.

Kafka, M. S., van Kammen, D. P., Kleinman, J. E., Nurnberger, J. I., Siever, L. J., Uhde, T. W., and Polinsky, R. J. 1980. Alpha-adrenergic receptor function in schizophrenia, affective disorders and some neurological diseases. *Communications in Psychopharmacology* 4:477–86.

Kafka, M. S., Wirz-Justice, A., and Naber, D. 1983. Circadian rhythms in rat brain neurotransmitter receptors. *Federation Proceedings* 42:2796–2801.

Kandell, E. R. 1983. From metapsychology to molecular biology: Explorations into the nature of anxiety. *American Journal of Psychiatry* 140:1277–93.

Klüver, H. 1933. *Behavior mechanisms in monkeys.* Chicago: University of Chicago Press.

—————. 1936. The study of personality and the method of equivalent and non-equivalent stimuli. *Character and Personality* 5:91–112.

Kohut, H. 1971. *The analysis of the self.* New York: International Universities Press.

Kris, E. 1952. *Psychoanalytic explorations in art.* New York: International Universities Press.

Laplanche, J., and Pontalis, J. B. 1967. *The language of psychoanalysis.* Translated by D. Nicholson-Smith. New York: Norton, 1973.

LeFever, H. 1961. To antipodes and back: Some observations on the LSD experience. Paper presented at Chestnut Lodge Symposium, Rockville, Maryland.

Lichtenstein, H. 1974. The effect of reality perception on psychic structure: A psychoanalytic contribution to the problem of the "generation gap." In *Annual of psychoanalysis*, vol. 2. New York: International Universities Press.

Lidz, T., and Fleck, S. 1960. Schizophrenia, human integration, and the role of the family. In *The etiology of schizophrenia*, edited by D. D. Jackson. New York: Basic Books.

Loewald, H. W. 1960. On the therapeutic action of psychoanalysis. *International Journal of Psycho-Analysis* 41:16–33.

—————. 1962. The superego and the ego ideal. II. Superego and time. *International Journal of Psycho-Analysis* 43:264–68.

—————. 1971. Some considerations on repetition and repetition compulsion. In *Papers on psychoanalysis.* New Haven: Yale University Press, 1980.

—————. 1979. The waning of the oedipus complex. In *Papers on psychoanalysis.* New Haven: Yale University Press, 1980.

Longuet-Higgins, H. C. 1968. The non-local storage of temporal information. *Proceedings of Royal Society, London* 171:327–34.

Longuet-Higgins, H. C., Willshaw, D. J., and Buneman, O. P. 1969. Non-holographic associative memory. *Nature* 222:960–62.

—————. 1970. Theories of associative recall. *Quarterly Review of Biophysics* 3:223–44.

Luby, E. D., Cohen, B. D., Rosenbaum, G., Gottlieb, J. S., and Kelley, R. 1959. Study of a new schizophrenomimetic drug— Sernyl. *AMA Archives of Neurology and Psychiatry* 81:363–69.

Malcolm, J. 1987, April 20. Reflections: J'appelle un chat un chat. *New Yorker*, pp. 84–102.

Mandell, A., Knapp, S., Ehlers, C., and Russo, P. 1982. The stability of constrained randomness: Lithium prophylaxis at several neurobiological levels. In *The neurobiology of the mood disorders*, edited by R. M. Post and J. C. Ballenger. Baltimore: Williams & Wilkins.

Meyer, J. S., Greifenstein, F., and Devault, M. 1959. A new drug causing symptoms of sensory deprivation. *Journal of Nervous and Mental Disease* 129:54–61.

Modell, A. 1968. *Object love and reality*. New York: International Universities Press.

Monod, J. 1972. *Chance and necessity*. New York: Random House.

Murray, H. A. 1938. *Explorations in personality*. New York: Oxford University Press.

Nagel, E., and Newman, J. R. 1958. *Gödel's proof*. New York: New York University Press.

Noble, D. 1951. A study of dreams in schizophrenia and allied states. *American Journal of Psychiatry* 107:612–16.

Novey, S. 1955. Some philosophical speculations about the concept of the genital character. *International Journal of Psycho-Analysis* 36:88–94.

Olson, D. H. 1969. Empirically unbinding the double-bind. Paper presented at the annual meeting of the American Psychological Association, Washington, D.C.

Ornstein, R. E. 1969. *On the experience of time*. Baltimore: Penguin Books.

Pollard, J. C., Bakker, C., Uhr, L., and Feuerfile, D. F. 1960. Controlled sensory input: A note on the technique of drug evaluation with a preliminary report on a comparative study of Sernyl, psilocybin and LSD-25. *Comprehensive Psychiatry* 1:377–80.

Pribram, K. H. 1986. The cognitive revolution and mind/brain issues. *American Psychologist* 41:507–20.

Prigogine, I. 1976. Order through fluctuation: Self-organization and social system. In *Evolution and consciousness: Human systems in transition*, edited by E. Jantsch and C. H. Waddington. Reading, Mass.: Addison-Wesley.

Rabin, M. 1977. *Handbook of mathematical logic, part C*. Amsterdam: North Holland.

Rabin, M., and Halpern, J. 1987. Logic to reason about likelihood. *Artificial Intelligence* 32, no. 3:379–405.

Rangell, L. 1981. From insight to change. *Journal of American Psychoanalytic Association* 29:119–41.

Rapaport, D. 1960. *The structure of psychoanalytic theory*. New York: International Universities Press.

Reiser, M. F. 1984. *Mind, brain, body: Toward a convergence of psychoanalysis and neurobiology*. New York: Basic Books.

Ringuette, E. L., and Kennedy, T. 1966. An experimental study of the double-bind hypothesis. *Journal of Abnormal Psychology* 71:136–41.

Rose, G. J. 1980. *The power of form: A psychoanalytic approach to aesthetic form*. New York: International Universities Press.

Rose, S. R. 1980. Can the neurosciences explain the mind? *Trends in Neurosciences* 23:2–4.

Ryder, R. G. 1966. Two replications of color matching factors. *Family Process* 5:43–48, 1966.

———. 1968. Husband-wife dyads versus married strangers. *Family Process* 7:233–38.

———. 1969. Three myths: Brief ruminations on interaction procedures while contemplating the color matching tests. Paper presented at the annual meeting of the National Council on Family Relations, Washington, D.C.

———. 1970. Dimensions of early marriage. *Family Process* 9:51–68.

Ryder, R. G., and Goodrich, D. W. 1966. Married couples' responses to disagreement. *Family Process* 5:30–42.

Ryder, R. G., Kafka, J. S., and Olson, D. H. 1971. Separating and joining influences in courtship and early marriage. *American Journal of Orthopsychiatry* 41:450–64.

Sandler, J., and Joffe, W. 1967. The tendency to persistence in psychological function and development, with special reference to fixation and regression. *Bulletin of the Menninger Clinic* 31:257–71.

Sandler, J., and Rosenblatt, B. 1962. The concept of the representational world. *Psychoanalytic Study of the Child* 17:128–45.

Sartre, J. P. 1960. *Search for a method*. Translated by H. E. Barnes. New York: Knopf, 1967.

Savage, C. 1955. Variations in ego feeling induced by d-lysergic acid diethylamide (LSD-25). *Psychoanalytic Review* 42:1–16.

Schachtel, E. G. 1947. On memory and childhood amnesia. *Psychiatry* 10:1–26.

Schilder, P. 1935. *The image and appearance of the human body*. New York: International Universities Press, 1950.

Schizophrenia costs U.S. billions; more research, better care needed. 1986, December 19. *Psychiatric News*, p. 8.

Schulz, C. G., and Kilgalen, R. K. 1969. The treatment course of a disturbed patient. In *Case studies in schizophrenia*. New York: Basic Books.

Searles, H. F. 1960. *The nonhuman environment in normal development and in schizophrenia*. New York: International Universities Press.

———. 1965. On driving the other person crazy. In *Collected papers on schizophrenia and related subjects*. New York: International Universities Press.

Smith, G. J. W., and Danielsson, A. 1982. Anxiety and defensive strategies in childhood adolescence. *Psychological Issues*, Monograph 52.

Smith, J. H. 1976. The psychoanalytic understanding of human freedom: Freedom from and freedom for. *Journal of the American Psychoanalytic Association* 26:87–107.

———. 1983. Rite, ritual and defense. *Psychiatry*. 46:16–30.

Squire, L. R. 1986, June 27. Mechanisms of memory. *Science* 232:1612–19.

Stein, M. I. 1949. Personality factors involved in temporal development of Rorschach responses. *Rorschach Research Exchange and Journal of Projective Techniques* 13:355–414.

Stierlin, H., Wynne, L. C., and Wirsching, M., eds. 1983. *Psychosocial intervention in schizophrenia*. Berlin: Springer-Verlag.

Stirnimann, F. 1947. Das Kind und seine früheste Umwelt. *Psychologische Praxis*, vol. 6. Basel: Karger.

Stone, L. 1986. Psychoanalytic observations on the pathology of depressive illness: Selected spheres of ambiguity or disagreement. *Journal of the American Psychoanalytic Association* 34:329–62.

Strachey, J. 1934. The nature of the therapeutic action of psychoanalysis. *International Journal of Psycho-Analysis* 15:127–59.

Thomä, H., and Kächele, H. 1987. *Principles*. Vol. 1 of *Psychoanalytic practice*. Translated by M. Wilson and D. Roseveare. New York: Springer-Verlag.

Turner, V. 1977. Process, system, and symbol: A new anthropological synthesis. *Daedalus* 106, no. 3:61–80.

Unger, S. M. 1963. Mescaline, LSD, psilocybin, and personality change: A review. *Psychiatry* 26:111–25.

Vonnegut, K., Jr. 1969. *Slaughterhouse-Five*. New York: Delta.

Wallerstein, R. S. 1973. Psychoanalytic perspectives on the problem of reality. *Journal of the American Psychoanalytic Association* 21:5–33.

Watzlawick, P., Beavin, J. H., and Jackson, D. 1967. *Pragmatics of human communication.* New York: W. W. Norton.

Westerlundh, B., and Smith, G. 1983. Percept-genesis and the psychodynamics of perception. *Psychoanalysis and Contemporary Thought* 6:597–640.

Whitehead, A. N., and Russell, B. 1910. *Principia mathematica.* Cambridge: Cambridge University Press.

Wilson, E. 1975. *Sociobiology.* Cambridge: Harvard University Press.

Winnicott, D. W. 1958a. Transitional objects and transitional phenomena. In *Collected Papers.* New York: Basic Books.

———. 1958b. Hate in the countertransference. In *Collected Papers.* New York: Basic Books.

Wynne, L. C., Ryckoff, I. M., Day, J., and Hirsch, S. I. 1958. Pseudomutuality in the family relations of schizophrenics. *Psychiatry* 21:205–20.

Index